PALEO DIET

By Ma

150 Recipes, The Secret Of Weight Loss

The Simple Science Of A Healthy Body In Paleo Way

Naturally fight diseases And Gain Maximum Energy

Table of Contents

Introduction

I want to thank you and congratulate you for downloading the book, "PALEO DIET FOR BEGINNERS: 150 RECIPES, The Secret Of Weight Loss, The Simple Science Of A Healthy Body In Paleo Way, Naturally fight diseases And Gain Maximum Energy ".

The paleo diet is great for a number of different things, such as longevity, weight loss, energising oneself as well as improving overall well-being. You could incorporate the paleo diet for these or any number of reasons, and so this book is a guide to help you on your way to attaining your goals. We'll take you step-by-step through how you could integrate the paleo lifestyle in an easy and effective manner.

This guide was designed for beginners and covers a wide range of questions and topics you may have about starting on this diet, including:

- What the paleo diet is and how it works in the context of health and improvement of well-being in all its detail.

- What ingredients and food choices can be considered as part of the paleo diet, which foods do not fit in the paleo category, which foods are in the grey area in between as well as what foods could be optionally added.
- An overview of how easily the paleo diet could be integrated into your lifestyle, including guides on how to eat the paleo way, how you could optimise the paleo diet to suit weight loss needs, how you could save a ton of money through eating paleo among a huge variety of other benefits.
- A huge selection of healthy, nutritious recipes for paleo that any beginner could do to get their foot in the door. Main meals, entrees, desserts, side dishes, you name it. From baked goods to smoothies and simplistic finger foods, you can get started on feeling better right away.

Everything a beginner may need to know before starting on the paleo diet is compiled quickly and easily, right here. No added filler or kerfuffle, and in a neat and orderly arrangement so that you won't get all turned around when looking for the things you need to know.

Once you're all done with this book, you're guaranteed to find it much simpler to incorporate the diet into your life than you may have thought at the beginning. This diet is incredibly energising, allows you to lose weight in a safe and healthy manner and you'll be feeling great in no time!

What are we waiting for? Jump right on in and let's get started!

Chapter 1 What exactly is the Paleo Diet?

Your body is naturally designed to filter out the bad stuff and toxins that you'll inevitably find entering your body through food and other external exposures. Food has evolved throughout the ages, but a little too quickly for our body's evolution to handle, and thus we're stuck with a whole lot of food, especially processed ones that our body was never meant to consume or handle.

Introducing the paleo diet! To put it simply, the paleo diet encompasses the foods that your body is evolutionarily designed to handle before food industries and society drastically skewed the change curve.

It is one of the only diets that keeps the human body happy without unnecessary starvation or unreasonable restrictions. Although you may not be used to the changes, your body is highly adapted and receptive to the kinds of foods you find on the paleo diet and will thus be kinder to you when you go about wanting to remain healthy and lean.

Explaining the basics using a simple metaphor

The paleo diet may yet be a foreign and strange concept to you, but let's break down its principles using a basic analogy, shall we?

Just say for an instance that you work at the zoo, and your particular responsibility involves keeping the animals happy and healthy as possible in their respective environments. Now external factors aside such as environment and individual temperaments, how could you go about doing this?

It's simple. Feed them the right foods! Their food is an essential factor in ensuring they develop as healthily as possible. The simplest solution is to feed them foods that they would normally find in the wild. Pandas are a prime example. They eat only bamboo shoots and variants thereof.

Pandas are a very interesting group of animals. Did you know that there is evidence that pandas used to eat quite a bit of meat in the ages gone by? Evolution has caused their diets to change from primarily omnivorous to that of herbivores over time, although evidence in their teeth are leftovers from what they used to eat. Of course, there have been some incidents in the modern day where pandas have been recorded eating a small amount of meat, but that is another story.

The main point of this is, pandas evolved to the point where their main energy source comes from bamboo-based vegetation, and if you were to feed them meats, their bodies are not adapted to eating that kind of food in bulk amounts. They wouldn't be able to survive, let along thrive.

The difference is not in the energy levels of the foods. You can have an equivalent energy output from consuming meats compared to vegetables, or vice versa. However, if your body is not adapted to using it as a source of energy, then you are going to get some backlash physiologically when you attempt to get your body to work with you – and this has been shown in weight loss studies and general health studies. Apply this technicality to humans, and you have the logic of why a paleo diet could have benefits for you.

Are modern diets so bad? What make them so?

Modern diets build their foundation and structure upon a new system, and that is agriculture. Humans have been farming for several thousands of years in some form or another in order to produce sustainable crops for consumption. However, in recent years with the advent of technological advances, farming became something that could be mass produced, and shipments of foods now circle about the globe, creating a bulk distribution pattern in places where there weren't before. Farming has its uses in helping to create a sustainable settlement of human civilisation, which allowed us to focus on higher pursuits above our body's physiological needs.

However, as our food rapidly changed, our bodies could not keep up with adjusting to fit modernised food types that we're exposed to now. In our advancements, we've created a roadblock in terms of how our bodies can adapt and evolve and so for many of us, it's still stuck in the evolutionary stage of hunter-gatherer society and thus is used to and optimised for those kinds of foods.

Consider it this way: if you were taking a 100 question test in elementary school, and although the first 99 questions were very straightforward and easy, the 100th question is at university grade level, and you freak out. That's how your body is reacting to modern food and the way agriculture has shifted the kinds of food we're exposed to.

This is significant because evolution hasn't taught our bodies fast enough how to adapt to modernised foods. We are seeing less veggies, fruit and seafood in our diets and instead have turned to a diet filled with refined grain, industrial vegetable oils and sweeteners.

Although the food itself is easy to create in large quantities and cheap to boot, they aren't what our body is designed to eat – an overall unhealthy choice compared to what's naturally designed for us.

Chapter 2 An overview of the paleo diet

Paleo is short for the Palaeolithic era from which hunter-gatherer human societies originated from. The foods that were commonplace for them are pretty similar throughout the world with only minor variances in the vegetation to account for climate differences.

Paleo diet uses these foods, or their modern equivalents in order for us to make the most of our food in terms of how efficient we are at extracting energy from it.

The foundations of the Paleo Diet were created from our ancestor's diet many years ago and these include foods such as nuts, seeds, vegetables, fruit, meat, seafood and certain types of roots.

With regards to meat, Hunter-Gatherer societies in the Palaeolithic era hunted for their meat. Animal meat was eaten quite often, and in several civilisations around the world in this era, many people made up the majority of their diet using fished meats among other kinds of hunted meats. Minerals, healthy fats, nutrients such as B-vitamins and protein are some of the main reasons meat and seafood allowed the civilizations to prosper. There've been almost no documented records of tribal cultures in the Palaeolithic era developing further without some kind of meat or animal-sourced food.

With considerations to seafood, almost all Palaeolithic humans who lived in that era have had some form of seafood, so long as they lived near bodies of water. Fish and other forms of seafood are a great source of protein, complex B vitamins, omega-3 fatty acids, selenium, zinc, iron, vitamin D and E as well as other elements such as phosphorus and magnesium. Antioxidants can also be found in most forms of seafood alongside other nutrients.

Fruits are a key source of minerals, vitamins and antioxidants. Humans also partook in gatherer behaviours which allowed them to collect fruits for food. They sourced fruits from anywhere they could gather it, however it wasn't a sustainable source because of seasonal availability. In the modern age, farmed fruits have been selectively bred to be high in carbohydrates as well as sugar, so eating in moderation is usually the key when it comes to modern fruits. Of course, fruit is a natural source of energy that was available in this era and so it finds a place in the Paleo Diet.

The human diet has turned vegetables and plant vegetation into one of the most optimal sources of nutrients throughout history. Vegetables in particular have a key place in the Paleo Diet due to its source of antioxidants, minerals, vitamins and other phytonutrients.

Nuts and seeds played a huge role in the nutrient-rich diet that the Palaeolithic era human beings had access to. Any tribe that could access them had found themselves a source of protein as well as healthy fats. Because of the presence of fats, individuals should consume these with care while on the Paleo Diet, as well as the fact that polyunsaturated fats were a limited resource for humans who lived in the Palaeolithic era. Even so this should not bar you from including some of it in your diet.

Roots are an interesting choice that Palaeolithic humans chose to include in their diet. Although roots may not be what you're expecting them to be. Roots can include starchy vegetables and tubers that are grown in the ground. Their high-carb content needs to be taken into account when taken in the modern paleo diet, so caution must be taken if you choose to include these. Nevertheless, roots and root vegetables are still a very good choice to obtain complex carbohydrates and healthy minerals and nutrients to complement the other parts of your diet.

In accordance with what foods are available today the modern Paleo Diet will include some foods that are and sisters only had access to every now and again such as honey (our ancestors wouldn't have had many opportunities to get them amidst the dangerous bees) as well as domesticated bird eggs (remember farming wasn't a Norm in this time period). Because you don't have to follow the Paleo diet to 80 just as a Palaeolithic hunter-gatherer would, and you didn't be afraid of them because they are both good choices for obtaining beneficial nutrients and compounds.

Most Paleo Diet guides will advise you and encourage you to take a good chunk of spices and herbs along with your foods. They add a unique taste to your meals and there is very little danger of it being overeaten. Human civilizations have been using herbs to spice up their meals for many years, whether for flavour purposes or health related purposes.

As for exceptions to the rule, there are some modern foods that are allowed to be eaten while on the paleo diet, but only in moderate amounts. These include chocolates, tea, healthy oils and coffee. Of course, agriculture is involved in the production of nearly all of these, but the processing it requires is normally not as bad as in other processed foods, such as refined grains and sugars as well as industrial vegetable oils. They also contain good and natural compounds that you would find another Palaeolithic foods, including but not limited to antioxidants and good fats.

It's important to remember that the purpose of going on the Paleo Diet is not about trying to re-create history. Times have changed that fact is indisputable. Instead, what we're trying to focus on is how we can use modern food sources in an optimal way, such that our bodies can use the fuel sources it was physiologically adapted to use. This is done by using a Hunter-Gatherer lifestyle diet as a guide. The Paleo Diet also has some scientific evidence to back it up.

Refined Sweeteners and sugars

You must have heard it time and time again, but let's make it clear once more. Sugars are bad for your health, and refined sugars more so. We apply the same principle in the Paleo Diet.

From a biological, evolutionary perspective, Hunter-Gatherer societies rarely ever had access to sugar in such large quantities as we do now in the modern day. The largest source of sugar for Hunter-Gatherer civilizations almost always came from fruits. Unlike modern fruits, these were fibrous and nutrient dense, as well as only being available seasonally. As we've mentioned before, modern fruits have also been bred to have higher sugar and carbohydrate concentrations compared to fruits of the past. Other forms of sugar such as honey were only available to those who had access to it due to their geographical location, and even then, access was very limited.

According to modern scientific studies, there's been a huge body of evidence suggesting that eating refined sugars and sweeteners could potentially:

- Dampen your body's white blood cell functionality and efficacy, which then lowers your body's aptitude of fighting off hard diseases.
- Reduce your body's leptin production – an appetite controlling hormone.
- Increases your body's oxidative stress states.
- Be linked to insulin resistance illnesses in large enough amounts. Insulin resistance is a key contributor to weight gain and fat storage processes in the short term. Diabetes and heart disease are also correlated with this health condition.

Chapter 3 Frequently Asked Questions

How different is the paleo diet compared to other diets?

The reason why the Paleo Diet has an advantage over other forms of diets is because it's more of a lifestyle shift. This means it's not meant to be a short-term thing in order to lose a bit of weight. The Paleo Diet is created to be a sustainable and healthy diet that you maintain over the long-term. It's not much of a stretch to say that you could enjoy nutritious and delicious paleo food for the rest of your life, and maintain all the benefits that come with it. This allows you to maintain an adequate level of mental focus, a healthy weight and a lean body, making yourself more energetic as well as reducing the onset of chronic diseases well into your elderly days. In this sense the diet is much more appealing to those who want a long-term change that will last them the rest of their life. Never falling back on junk food again will give you a new lease on life!

Most of the conventional diets don't take into account what your body was designed to eat naturally, and so as we've said before the Paleo Diet usually takes into account what our body is naturally adapted to using as fuel. You can't argue with that!

But I need fibres and nutrients from grains, and everyone keeps saying that whole grains are the new superfood. If I cut grains out of my Paleo diet, won't I be missing out?

We talked about grains before, and we said that whole grains are usually not that great of a source for minerals, B vitamins and fibre compared to seafood, veggies and fruits. Compare this: a 1000 calorie serve of vegetables and fruits has anywhere from 2-7 times the fibre compared to a similar serve of whole grains. The stats for micronutrients is pretty similar as well, with vegetables and fruits sometimes having 10-15 times more calcium, and multiple times more potassium, magnesium, iron and various other minerals compared to whole grains.

What's more lectins and phytates can often be found in all grains, these compounds can be harmful to your digestive system through a rotation and nutrient absorption interference. Some studies have also linked these compounds to inflammation processes that could be damaging.

You can obtain more information on why the Paleo Diet considers conventional, whole grains to be unhealthy in our section on non-paleo foods. However what you need to grasp at the moment is grains aren't the best source for these nutrients that you need, and you can obtain just as many, if not more, from just the right selection of vegetables and fruits.

How can the paleo diet help me lose weight?

The Paleo Diet is great at making a person more it healthier but is also a great way to efficiently lose weight. This is because the Paleo Diet has a good amount of wholefood protein, natural fats, and nutrients and is also low sugar. All this player hand in weight loss benefits on paleo diet.

- Protein increases your metabolism for more effective fat burning. It has two to three times the thermic effect of carbs and fat. Proteins are also more satisfying when comparing on the calorie to calorie basis of carbohydrates and fats. This means that you can eat less protein for the same amount of satiation compared to the same amount of carbohydrates and fat.
- Despite proteins being a bit more satiating, healthy and natural fats are more satisfying compared to processed carbohydrates and grains that are present in most people's diets. Hormone balances also kept in check, alongside your mood, blood sugar and appetite.
- A micronutrient-rich diet sends a message to your body that it's getting adequate nutrition and therefore unnecessary hunger pangs do not trouble you as much as it does before in order for you to take in more nutrients (as it does when you fill your diet with empty calories).
- A diet that's low in sugar and simple carbohydrates allows you to maintain an adequate level of sugar and energy levels throughout your

working day. This also plays a part in preventing sugar cravings that leads to overeating foods that are filled with empty calories.

All these factors pay contributions to allow the paleo diet to be very effective when it comes to weight loss. What's more, the Paleo Diet as a natural appetite reduction effect. Most individuals will be able to lose weight without having to resort to tedious tasks such as maintaining a food diary or minding their food portions or counting calories. Sounds great, right? On the contrary, there are a large number of high-carb, low-fat diets which make you feel terribly hungry most of the time, but also require record keeping to boot. Paleo sounds much better!

To put it simply not only is the Paleo diet very effective for optimising your energy levels health and longevity, but it is also a long term method for sustainable and effective weight loss.

Is paleo a good choice for everyone?

Because of its nature The Paleo Diet has intrinsic anti-inflammatory properties. It's also a great source of antioxidants healthy fats proteins and micronutrients. What's more, the nature of the diet allows you to maintain low sugars and processed refined flours, processed foods and hydrogenated veggie oils. With all these factors that means that this is one of the best diets that can effectively lower your risk of developing many of the so-called diseases of civilization including diabetes, heart disease, and Alzheimer's.

 Among these larger health benefits there are some people that have reported smaller Earth it's such as with gastric issues,   acid reflux, acne, and indigestion. Since it also is a great way to lose weight, all the benefits of weight loss go with it.

Take into consideration that if you do have a diagnosed health condition, simply going on the Paleo Diet will most likely not cure you. So long as you work with your doctor and other health professionals through any changes in your lifestyle or your diet, you should be just fine. Don't stop taking the treatments and medications that are required for your condition. So long as you're being supervised by your doctor or an appropriate health professional, you might find use yet in the Paleo Diet when it comes to improving the condition of your chronic disease.

Reference guide to Paleo Food

The principle for the diet is simple. By allowing yourself only the foods that were available during the Palaeolithic era and cutting out unnecessary food sources from the modern day, you give yourself an overall better health outcome.

"Easier said than done!" You might say. Completely understandable. In the modern day and age we get our foods from the grocers, and even with a guide in mind, it becomes a little bit difficult to find what you're looking for. In this section, we'll provide you with an easy and simple list of foods to start off with. We've also explained why each food group is in the category that it's in.

There will still be some grey area as to whether or not the food is paleo or not. This knowledge is important if you want to categorise it in the broader picture of your personal paleo diet. Any questions that you have should be able to be answered right here in this section.

If you're a beginner, take it easy and relax. You needn't overwhelm yourself with a whole bunch of information right away. You don't need to know everything in this section in order to get started. For now, what you want to focus on is identifying which foods are paleo and which are not. If you just want to get down to the bones of things, you can go ahead and skip past the detailed explanations and skip on over to the next chapter to begin right away. Once you are through with that, feel free to come back and process the information in this section at your own pace.

Quick Reference List

Paleo Foods

- Seeds and nuts
- Spices and herbs
- Fruits
- Natural and healthy oils (coconut/olive oil are good examples)
- Eggs
- Roots (squash, yams, and starchy tubers)
- Meats (seafood, poultry).
- Leafy green veggies (not starch-based)
- Paleo sweeteners (maple syrup and honey)

Non-Paleo Foods

- Dairy
- Alcohol
- Refined sugars (cane sugars and corn syrup)
- Grain (soy, rice and corn)
- Potatoes
- Legumes and beans

- Artificial sweeteners (e.g. sucralose and aspartame)
- Industrial veggie oils and seeds (e.g. soybean and canola oil)

Semi-Paleo Foods

- Fruit juices
- Tea and coffee
- Paleo natural sweeteners (honey/maple syrup)
- Nightshade veggies
- Butter from Grass-fed cows
- Paleo artificial sweeteners (xylitol and stevia)

Chapter 4 Categorizations of Specific Food Groups

Paleo Foods

Meat

Meat could be considered one of the foundational pillars of the paleo diet since it made up such a huge and integral part of our ancestor's diet. Red meats are included in this selection, which is normally classified as unhealthy by a lot of health groups – and within this greater group, it includes options from the common beef to rarer meats such as bison and lamb. This meat category also encompasses the various forms of seafood, including shellfish, molluscs and a variety of fish. Red meats should optimally come from animals that have been fed grass in the pasture, and seafood is best when caught through conventional fishing and not through fish farming.

Eggs

In the Palaeolithic era, the average human would have almost never eaten eggs unless they came across a bird nest with eggs on the chance occasion. When comparing nutritional status, eggs are about on par with the benefits of meats – if you take into consideration their high protein and micronutrient contents. In the modern day, the eggs that you'd find most commonly are chicken eggs, but other bird eggs including those from ducks, pheasants and quails are also just as healthy. Just like with your red meats, eggs should be obtained from birds raised free-range or in a pasture.

Vegetables

Since sugary plant-based foods like some fruits and nuts are off the menu, vegetables should make up a large part of your paleo diet's foundations. Starchy root vegetables are one option in this category, but take caution with the amount you consume due to high carb concentrations.

Fruit

Fruits are highly nutritious and delicious, which make them a joy to add to the paleo diet. Considering, though, that fruits contain a sizeable portion of natural sugars, they should only be eaten in moderate amounts to prevent carb and sugar overload. Modern fruits in particular are some of the worst offenders when it comes to sugar content due to selective breeding over the ages.

Once you've taken this into account, it brings you down to the recommendation of only a few servings of fruit per day. You can also reduce your sugar intake overall by making the choice to consume low-sugar fruit varieties, such as berries. Berries are a good option if you're watching your caloric intake, and a healthier alternative to other modern-day fruits due to the added effect of antioxidants – especially in dark berry varieties.

Beginners to the paleo diet should limit themselves to anything around 2-3 servings daily. This is also a good guideline to have for those maintaining a healthy weight. Those who are using carb-restrictive diets however, may also want to reduce their fruit intake a little bit more.

Tubers (starchy root vegetables)

Starchy root veggies provide a good source of complex carbohydrates that take longer to digest – and thus keeps you fuller for longer. They have a decent amount of minerals and vitamins as well. Antioxidants are abundant in darker-coloured root vegetables, while orangey types like sweet potato are high in carotenoids, including Vitamin A. The purple, Okinawan, sweet potatoes, however, are chock-full of antioxidants called anthocyanin (the same sort you can find in blueberries).

Nuts and Seeds

As we've said before, seeds and nuts are something that should be eaten in moderation, but the right amounts could easily make or break the diet.

Let's consider it as a whole. Overall, the benefits of seeds and nuts outweigh the cons by a fair margin. Given that it has a favourable nutritional profile – with an all-around inclusion of carbs, good fats, proteins, vitamin E antioxidants and a wide variety of minerals, they make for a good complement to the rest of your diet.

Be aware and take caution if you find yourself overeating these products, especially if they come in the forms of nut-based flours or butters. Limit yourself to only a few servings each day to prevent health detriments you could get from indulging too much.

Herbs and Spices

The paleo diet works perfectly well with any number of spices, herbs and seasonings – even salt! At almost no time in history has there ever been food preparation without them, whether for flavouring food better or to be used for medicinal purposes. For as long as humans have been using them, there has been little record of detrimental effects, which means it's most likely safe for inclusion on the paleo diet.

Healthy Oils

Oils are a bit of an odd group on the surface. You've most likely been told of the health effects of olive oil. However, if we are to look at this from a paleo point of view, we see that Palaeolithic humans had almost no exposure to purified oils. You might ask, 'so what oils are safe on the paleo diet?'

We'll give you a list as a guide to what could be considered safe for paleos:

- Fish oil
- Avocado oil
- Sesame oil
- Olive oil
- Coconut oil
- Palm oil
- Flax seed oil
- Nut oils such as walnut, hazelnut, almonds and macadamia

Natural Sweeteners

There are several natural sweeteners that are safe for individuals on the paleo diet to take, including maple syrup and honey. Both sweeteners can be used in place of one another when it comes to flavouring a meal, although their nutritional profiles and origins differ. If you're still not sure, we'll list out the factors of these two sweeteners on their own, and while we're at it, explain a little bit more about others you may encounter!

Honey

It's a bit of a controversial food option when it comes to the paleo diet. As it is a completely natural food source, there have been human tribes that have access to honey throughout the ages. However, by looking at its nutrient profile, it's composed almost entirely of sugar, which may destroy the principles of what the paleo diet usually is – which is the low-carb aspect.

Maple Syrup

Just like honey, maple syrup is almost completely made up of sugars, but in comparison to artificial sweeteners, this option is a much healthier option by far.

Stevia

Stevia has gained plenty of traction and attention as a sweetener with a very low calorie profile. It has gained uses outside of the paleo diet as a replacement for aspartame and sucralose – which are normally used in mass produced products. As the source of stevia stems from a South American plant, it is purely a natural sweetener that can be bought in either a liquid or powder form.

Coffee and tea

Strictly speaking, tea and coffee are not classified as paleo beverages. This is because you wouldn't have found a coffee machine or a teakettle back in the Palaeolithic era! However, there is enough evidence to suggest that a moderate consumption of these drinks may actually be beneficial to your health.

Paleo Weight Loss Strategies

The paleo diet is created as a way to improve your lifestyle with all the added benefits of energy, longevity and mental acuity. There have been countless people who have tried the paleo diet for reasons other than losing weight, yet they lose weight in the process without any extra effort! This is because the paleo diet is high-protein, high in good fats and low in carbs, while being extremely nutritious.

Once paleo has become routine for you, and you want further weight loss effects added on top of the health benefits you'll have no doubt gained from the diet, you can implement a few techniques to optimise the fat burning process. This boils down to one principle, and that is to limit your carbs as much as possible.

Measuring carbs

The targets that you would aim for in terms of daily consumption are quantified in grams per day. These targets are more of a guideline than a set rule, which means you don't have to undergo the tedium of managing a diary recording how much you've had that day. In weight loss, this management isn't particularly important.

Eat more fat and protein

Once you've cut most carbs from your diet, you're halfway there. Protein and fat intake in adequate amounts will handle the rest of the work. Protein intake in particular should be increased, which shouldn't be too difficult for you to do. In fact, there is a school of thought that believes that the mechanism of low-carb diets is accepted by the body and your body adapts to this change by naturally using more proteins and fats to convert to energy in place of what would normally be carbs.

Low Intensity Exercise

You don't have to go full out pumping at the gym to see any benefits like many other weight loss plans tell you to do. In fact, low-to-moderate exercise should do the trick. Studies have shown a number of benefits with low-intensity exercise, and these include:

- A reduction in excess systemic inflammation responses.
- A strengthening of the immune system.
- Bettering an individual's well-being and mood – perfect for combating depression.
- Helping the body burn fat better.

- Lowering the risk of developing chronic illnesses, including those associated with the heart and your metabolism.
- Strengthening your heart functionality
- Reinforcing your bone, muscle and joint strength – of particular use in the elderly – allowing for higher intensity exercise in the future

Best of luck on your diet!

Chapter 5 PALEO BREAKFAST RECIPES

Yummy Chia Seeds Orange Granola

Ingredients:

2 cups raw almonds

1 cup raw sunflower seeds

¼ cup chia seeds

2 tbsp orange zest

¼ cup olive oil

1 cup chopped dried apricots

1 cup raw pumpkin seeds

1 cup coconut flakes

1 tbsp ground vanilla bean

½ cup pure maple syrup

¼ cup apple butter

Instructions:

Preheat oven at 275 degrees.

Add almonds to your food processor and blend until it is broken into smaller pieces. Place it in a large bowl. Add the remaining ingredients except for the apricots. Stir well with a spoon and make sure that it is coated. Spread the mixture on top of two baking sheets.

Bake for 30 minutes. Stir it three times every 10 minutes. Continue to bake until it is golden brown. Remove it then pour in a bowl. Chop the apricots into very small pieces. Add it to the bowl and stir to coat. Let it cool then store in a container.

Nutrition Information: 350 calories, 23 g fat, 26 g net carbs, 12 g protein

Tomato Scrambled Eggs

Ingredients:

- 2 tbsp. avocado oil
- 6 beaten eggs
- 4 wedged tomatoes
- 2 sliced green onions

Instructions:

In a large skillet, heat 1 tbsp. of your avocado oil on medium heat. Once heated, cook your eggs while stirring with a silicone spatula until they are almost cooked. Once almost cooked, slide your eggs on to a plate.

Now, add the rest of your avocado oil to the skillet and cook your tomatoes until most of the liquid has gone. Now, put your eggs back in the skillet and add in your green onions. Stir these ingredients all together for 45 seconds or so until your eggs are cooked through.

Nutrition Information: 264 calories, 18 g fat, 9.2g carbs, 14.5 g protein

Garlic Turkey Burger

Ingredients:

1 pound ground turkey

4 eggs

1 tbsp. olive oil

¼ cup chopped red onion

½ tsp garlic powder

½ tsp pepper

¼ tsp oregano

Directions:

1. Combine the ground turkey, red onion, pepper, garlic powder, oregano together in a bowl.

2. Prepare 4 patties with a whole in the middle, like a donut shape, but a large whole.

3. Heat olive oil in a skillet.

4. Cook your burger patties well on each side. A few minutes before the meat is done, crack an egg in each burger middle and cook.

Nutrition Information: 355 calories, 11.5 g fat, 7.5carbs, 35g protein

Brussel Sprouts Bacon

Ingredients:

2 cups Tbsp.

2 cups shredded Brussels sprouts

2 eggs

1 minced garlic clove

1 tsp. cumin

1 tsp. cayenne pepper

2 cooked slices of turkey bacon

2 eggs

1 Bartlett pear cut into small cubes or sweet apple of your choice

Directions:

1.   Heat the coconut oil in a skillet. Cook the onion, cumin, and the shredded Brussels sprouts for a few minutes.

2.   Add the pear or apple and cook another 3 or 4 minutes.

3.   When the fruits and veggies are cooked enough, crumble the cooked turkey bacon, and fry some eggs to place on top.

4.   Add some cayenne pepper to taste.

Nutrition Information: 195 Cal, 10.5 g fat , 6.5 g carb, 15g protein.

Favorite Scone

Ingredients:

2 cups coconut flour

½ tsp. baking soda

¼ cup dried raisins and ¼ cup dried apricots

¼ cup sunflower seeds and ¼ cup pumpkin seeds

¼ cup chopped walnuts

1 egg

2 tbsp. maple syrup

Directions:

1. Combine the coconut flower, baking soda and dried fruits. Add the nuts next, and mix well.

2. In a different bowl, mix the egg and the maple syrup.

3. Stir the wet ingredients into the dry mixture.

4. Form a square shape, ¾"thick. Then make 12-16 scones.

5. Bake on a greased cooking sheet for 12 minutes or so.

Nutrition Information : 185 Cal, 6.5 g total fat, 0 mg chol, 12.5 g carb., 3g protein.

Combination Spicy Omelette

Ingredients:

4 eggs

1 avocado

1 chopped green onion

½ tsp. dried cilantro

2 Tbsp., salsa Verde (your favorite brand or even better homemade if you can)

1 tsp. lime juice

Black pepper

Directions:

1.   In a bowl, smash the avocado, salsa Verde, lime juice, cilantro and green onion. Set aside.

2.   Wisk your eggs and add some black pepper.

3.   Cook the eggs in a skillet with a drop of olive oil. Make sure you cook your eggs as 2 flat omelets you will be able to fold.

4.   Once cooked, plate the omelets and fill with the avocado mixture. You could choose to fill the omelet right in the skillet so the avocado filling can warm up. Serve and enjoy

Nutrition Information : 370 Cal, 12 g total fat, 305 mg chol, 7 g carb., 17g protein.

Healthy Paleo Granola

Ingredients:

½ cup melted grass feed butter

½ cup water

1/3 cup maple syrup

1 1/2 coconut flakes

1 ½ flaxseed meal

2 cups chopped walnuts

½ cup chopped pine nuts

½ cup sunflower seeds

½ cup pumpkin seeds

½ cup chopped cashews

1 tsp. ground cinnamon

1 tsp. sea salt

Directions:

1. Preheat oven to 250ºF.

2. In a bowl, combine the flaxseed meal, coconut flakes, sunflower seeds, pumpkin seeds, sea salt and cinnamon. Stir together well.

3. In a measure cup, mix the melted grass fed butter, water and maple syrup and stir together. Pour this liquid mix over the dry ingredients above and stir until everything is just slightly moist.

4. On a greased baking sheet (or with parchment sheet), place the mixture as an even layer. Bake for an over at 250 F.

5. Once cooked, remove and set aside.

6. Finally, place all the nuts on that same baking sheet (pine nuts, cashews, walnuts). Bake for 20 minutes or so.

7. You might need to repeat that process twice or until the nuts are roasted to your preference.

8. Finally, mix everything together, you should be left with chunks of seeds/syrup and roasted nuts.

9. Serve and enjoy.

Nutrition Information : 380 Cal, 25g total fat , 12g carb., , 8g protein.

Almond Carrot pancakes

Ingredients:

1 ½ cups almond flour

½ cup butter of choice

6 eggs

1 ½ tsp baking soda

2 ½ tsp ginger

2/3 cup coconut milk

1/3 cup coconut flour

½ cup applesauce or agave

½ tsp salt

2 tbsp cinnamon

1 ½ tsp nutmeg

2 cups finely shredded carrots

Directions:

Place all of the ingredients in a large bowl and whisk to combine. The batter
should be thick. Heat the pan over medium heat until it reaches about 300
degrees. Coat the pan with the cooking spray. Pour half cup of the batter on the
pan. Spread it into a circle and cook for 2 minutes on the first side before
flipping it. Cook for one minute on the other side. Feel free to cook it a little bit
more if it looks undone. Eat plain or with butter.

Nutrition Information: 85 calories, 5 g fat, 3.5 g net carbs, 4 g protein

Delicious Chicken Sausages

Ingredients:

1 ½ pound ground chicken

Olive oil

1 tsp. onion powder

½ tsp. ground nutmeg

½ tsp. dried turmeric

½ tsp. dried sage

½ dried rosemary

Directions:

1.   Combine all ingredients together in a bowl, expect the olive oil.

2.   Form 8-10 patties, the size you prefer (not as big as burger patties).

3.   Cook the meat in olive oil in a skillet, on medium heat. Make sure the patties are cooked thoroughly, probably 10 minutes or so on each side.

Nutrition Information   : 200 Cal, 15g total fat,   6g carb, 18g protein

Delight Stuffed Peppers

Ingredients:

4 slices of cooked turkey bacon

4 eggs

2 bell peppers (yellow, orange or red) – cut in halves and seeded

1 cup of chopped fresh asparagus

1 cup fresh sliced mushrooms

1 tsp. dried thyme

Salt and pepper

Directions:

1.   Preheat the oven to 375 F.

2.   Prepare al the veggies and in a bowl mix the eggs, cooked bacon, veggies, and seasonings.

3.   On a baking sheet, place the halves seeded and cleaned bell peppers face up.

4.   Fill the peppers with the eggs mixture.

5.   Cook in the oven for about 40 minutes.

Nutrition Information : 210 Cal, 10g total fat, 12g carb., 14.5g protein

Easy Cranberries Banana Muffins

Ingredients:

3 ripe bananas

4 eggs

½ cup almond flour

½ melted coconut oil

½ cup dried cranberries

1 tsp baking soda

1 tsp. baking powder

1 tsp vanilla extract

1 tsp cinnamon

Directions:

1.   Preheat the oven to 350 F.

2.   Prepare the muffins cups by greasing them individually.

3.   In a bowl mix the bananas, eggs, coconut oil, and vanilla. Blend well.

4.   Add the almond flour and the dried cranberries, baking soda, baking powder and cinnamon to the eggs mixture.

5.   Pour into the 12 muffins cups.

6.   Bake 20-25 minutes.

7.   Serve and Enjoy

Nutrition Information : 170 Cal, 5g total fat ,32g carb., 3g protein

Parsley Eggs in Avocados

Ingredients:

- 1 halved and pitted avocado

- 2 eggs

- 2 crumbled cooked bacon slices

- 2 tsp. fresh chopped chives

- 1 pinch dried parsley

- Sea salt and black pepper to taste

Directions:

Pre-heat your oven to 425 degrees.

While your oven pre-heats, crack your eggs in to a small mixing bowl.

Now, take a baking dish large enough to fit both halves of your avocado. Set your avocados skin side down and VERY carefully spoon the yolks of your eggs in to the holes in the center of the avocado halves. Fill the rest of the avocado hole with the egg white.

Once you have filled the centers of both of your avocados, sprinkle each egg filled avocado with your parsley, chives, salt and pepper.

When your oven has preheated, bake your egg filled avocados for 15 minutes or until your eggs are cooked through. When cooked completely, put your bacon on top of each avocado half and serve.

Nutrition Information: 248calories, 18.5 g fat, 9.2carbs, 9g protein

Butternut Squash Oatmeal

Ingredients:

- 1 halved butternut squash seeded

- ¼ cup coconut milk

- ½ tsp. cinnamon

- 1 tbsp. chopped walnuts

- Water

Directions:

Begin by pre-heating your oven to 350 degrees.

While your oven preheats, add ¼" water to a baking dish that is large enough to fit your butternut squash halves. Place your halves of butternut squash in the water in the dish skin side down.

Once your oven is pre-heated, cook your squash until it is soft – this should take about an hour.

Once cooked, take the squash out of the oven and let it cool.

Once your squash has cooled, scoop out the middle of the squash and put it in a breakfast bowl. Use a fork to mash up the squash and when it has a smooth consistency, add your cinnamon and coconut milk and mix it all together. Once mixed, sprinkle your walnuts on top and serve!

Nutrition Information: 242calories,6g fat, 4.9carbs, 4.9g protein

Almond Lemon and Blueberry Muffins

Ingredients:

- 3 room temperature eggs
- ½ cup melted coconut oil
- ¼ cup coconut sugar
- 1 zested lemon
- 1 tsp. lemon extract
- ¾ tsp. sea salt
- ½ tsp. baking soda
- ¼ tsp. baking powder
- 1 ½ cups almond meal
- 1 cup blueberries
- ½ cup melted coconut butter (for glaze)
- ½ cup raw honey (for glaze)
- 1 juiced lemon (for glaze)

Directions:

Begin by pre-heating your oven to 350 degrees.

While your oven pre-heats line a 12 cup muffin pan with paper liners.

In a mixing bowl, combine your lemon extract, coconut sugar, lemon zest, coconut oil and eggs and whisk together until well combined.

Over a clean bowl, using a sieve, sieve your baking powder, salt, baking soda together. Next, stir your almond meal in to this dry mixture.

Once your almond meal mixture is well combined, slowly mix in your wet mixture until you get a smooth batter.

Using a silicone spatula, gently fold your blueberries in to the batter.

Next, scoop your batter in to the paper muffin liners, filling each of them ¾ full to leave room for expansion.

Put your muffins in to the oven once it is preheated and bake for 30 minutes or until cooked through.

Once your muffins have cooked through and cooled, take a clean bowl and whisk together your honey, coconut butter and lemon juice for your glaze. When these ingredients are smooth, drizzle it over your cool muffins!

Nutrition Information: 279calories,16g fat, 25g carbs, 8g protein

Asparagus Ham Burrito

Ingredients:

2-4 slices of ham (not too thin)

2 egg whites

6 cooked asparagus spears

1 tbsp. olive oil

½ copped yellow onion

1 minced clove garlic

Salt, pepper

Directions:

1.   After cooking the asparagus is cooked. Set them aside, keep warm.

2.   In a skillet heat the olive oil and cook the onion and garlic.

3.   Beat the egg whites, salt and pepper and cook them also in the skillet with the veggies.

4.   Place the ham slices on the plate, fill with the egg mixture and asparagus.

5.   Roll the ham as you would a burrito. Serve with hot sauce if you like.

Nutrition Information : 205 Cal, 17.5 g total fat, 6.5 g carb, 21g protein.

Spinach Egg Breakfast

Ingredients:

2 large eggs

2 Tbsp. soy milk

1 cup chopped spinach

Salt and pepper

Olive oil

Directions:

1.   First, put in your blender the spinach, the eggs and the soy milk, mix well.

2.   Heat oil in skillet and cook these scrambled eggs.

3.   Serve with bacon, ham, or sausage.

Nutrition Information : 205 Cal, 17.5 g total fat ,, 6.5 g carb, 21g protein.

Paleo Garlic Mexican Chilaquiles

Ingredients:

2 tbsp ghee

2 garlic cloves, minced

4 Oz diced green chilies

Half sweet onion, diced

1 cup organic chicken broth

2 tbsp adobo sauce

3 eggs

1 cup organic chicken broth

2 cups sweet potato chips

2 radishes, thinly sliced

½ cup salsa

2 parsley sprigs, sliced

Directions:

Set the oven to 375 degrees.

Place your pan over medium heat. Use a pan without plastic handle since you will be placing this in your oven.

Cook the onion and garlic for a few minutes. Mix in the broth, green chilies and adobo sauce. Stir well to combine. Reduce heat and allow it to simmer. Add the sweet potato chips and stir to coat.

Set it aside to let the chips absorb the liquid. You can also add the chips small quantities at a time. Stir one last time to ensure that everything is well coated. Season it with salt and pepper.

Break the eggs on top of the mixture. Cook in the oven for 10-14 minutes. It is done when most of the liquid is absorbed. Garnish with the salsa, radish and parsley.

Nutrition Information: 436 calories, 27 g fat, 25 g net carbs, 16 g protein

Onion Breakfast Quiche

Ingredients:

1 cup raw cashews

4 cups spring greens, loosely packed

Half lime

8 eggs

1 cup roasted tomatoes, diced

½ tsp salt

1/8 tsp garlic powder

½ cup water

1 tbsp red onion, finely diced

1 tbsp olive oil

8 slices turkey bacon

1 tbsp green chilies, diced

½ tsp black pepper

Directions:

Soak the cashews in a bowl of water at room temperature. Set it aside for 4 hours. Drain the cashews and place it in a blender. Add half cup of fresh water and process the mixture until smooth.

Preheat your oven until it reaches 350 degrees. Cook the bacon then crumble into smaller pieces. Set it aside.

Heat olive oil in the pan and cook the onion, spring greens and lime juice. Cook for 3-5 minutes until the green are onions are wilted.

 Remove it from the heat and dice into small pieces. Mix the bacon, greens, tomatoes, spices, eggs, green chilies and cashew cream in a large bowl. Coat the bake pan with a cooking spray.

Pour the batter and spread evenly. Bake for 45 minutes until it is set. Serve with Greek yogurt, avocado or cilantro.

Nutrition Information: 257 calories, 18 g fat, 11 g net carbs, 12 g protein

Cinnamon Paleo Pancakes

Ingredients:

- 1 mashed banana
- 3 eggs
- ¼ cup almond flour
- 1 tbsp. almond butter
- 1 tsp. vanilla extract
- ½ tsp. cinnamon
- 1/8 tsp. baking soda
- 1/8 tsp. baking powder
- 1 tsp olive oil

Directions:

In a mixing bowl, combine your almond butter, banana, almond flour, eggs, vanilla extract, baking soda, cinnamon, and baking powder. Use a whisk to whisk together your ingredients until you get a smooth batter.

Next, add your olive oil to a skillet and heat over medium-high on your stovetop. Once warm, scoop your batter in to your skillet as if you were making traditional pancakes.

Cook your pancakes until you see bubbles in the center, then flip and cook until the other side is browned as well.

Cook all of your pancakes and serve warm with your favorite paleo friendly syrup or topping!

Nutrition Information: 120 calories,7.4g fat, 8.3g carbs, 8.3g protein

Honey Almond Granola

Ingredients:

2 cups slivered almonds

1 cup sunflower seeds

¼ tsp salt

4 tbsp honey

1 cup cherries, dried

1 cup pecans, chopped

1 cup unsweetened shredded coconut

2 tbsp coconut oil, melted

1 tsp vanilla extract

Directions:

Set the oven at 300 degrees.

Mix in the coconut, nuts and salt in a large mixing bowl. Stir to combine. Add the honey, vanilla and coconut oil in a smaller bowl. Whisk to combine then pour over the nut mixture.

Spread the mixture on top of a cookie sheet. Bake for 15-20 minutes until it is golden brown. Add in the dried cherries. Stir to combine and allow it cool before serving.

Nutrient Information: 337 calories, 22 g fat, 26 g net carbs, 7 g protein

Cinnamon Banana Porridge

Ingredients:

2 ripe bananas, mashed

1 ½ cup almond milk

¼ cup flax seed

½ almond meal

1 tsp. cinnamon

2 tbsp. guava syrup

Directions:

1.   Combine all ingredients in a medium pot and let it simmer for 10 minutes.

2.   It will thicken and you can add your favorite fresh fruits and coconut flakes.

Nutrition Information per serving: 205 Cal, 12.5 g total fat .11.5 g carb, 26g protein.

Coconut Zucchini Cakes

Ingredients:

1 large fresh Zucchini

2 ounces almond flour

3 eggs

A pinch of nutmeg

Coconut oil

Directions:

1.   Using a potatoes peeler, shred the zucchini in small strips

2.   In a bowl, mix all the ingredients.

3.   In a skillet heat some coconut oil and pour enough mixture to make your first pancake. Cook a few minutes on each side, until golden.

4.   Repeat the operation until all mixture is done. Serve and enjoy

Nutrition Information per serving: 65 Cal, 3.5 g total fat,4.5 g carb., 2g fiber, 4g protein.

Paleo Breakfast Salad

Ingredients:

2 eggs

2 cups of your favorite mixed greens

3 Tbsp. olive oil (2 for dressing and one for cooking)

1 minced garlic clove

½ tsp. Dijon mustard

A handful of black olives

Salt and pepper

Directions:

1.   In a bowl mix 2 Tbsp. olive oil, Dijon mustard, garlic, salt pepper. Set aside.

2.   Heat 1 Tbsp. olive oil in skillet.

3.   Crack the 2 eggs and cook, leaving yolks a little runny.

4.   On your bed of mixed greens place the eggs and the black olives.

5.   Serve with salad dressing on top.

Nutrition Information : 225 Cal, 20 g total fat , 3.2 g carb., , 7g protein.

Healthy Macadamia waffles

Ingredietns:

5 eggs

½ cup coconut milk

3 tbsp coconut oil, melted

¾ tsp baking soda

½ tsp salt

1 cup raw macadamia nuts

3 tbsp honey

3 tbsp coconut flour

½ tsp vanilla extract

For the syrup:

2 peaches, pitted and sliced

½ cup cherries, pitted

½ tsp vanilla extract

2 plums, pitted and sliced

¼ cup honey

½ tsp lemon juice

Directions:

Place the syrup ingredients in a small saucepan. Heat it until it simmers. Keep it at low heat to bring out the flavor of the fruit and make the liquid thick. Prepare the waffles. Preheat the waffle iron.

Place all of the ingredients in a blender. Blend for 30 seconds then increase the strength. Blend until the mixture is smooth. Slowly transfer the batter to the waffle iron and spread it evenly with a spoon. Cook the waffle for 45 seconds to one minute. Serve the waffle with the syrup. Serve warm.

Nutrient Information : 421 calories, 31 g fat, 28 g net carbs, 8 g protein

Tomato Chipotle Mini Meatloaves

Ingredients:

1 lb fresh chorizo, casings removed

2 tbsp adobo sauce

¾ cup almond flour

5 cloves garlic, diced

1 lb ground beef

2 eggs, wild range

1 large onion, diced

Tallow

For the sauce:

1 oz chipotle in adobo sauce

2 cups cilantro, chopped

1 lime

1 pint cherry tomatoes

2 tbsp olive oil

½ tsp salt

Half avocado

Directions:

Set the oven at 350 degrees. Cook the garlic and onion until it is soft. Place half of the onion and garlic mixture in a bowl and the other half in food processor. Place the almond flour, ground beef, adobo sauce, chorizo and egg to the bowl of onion and garlic. Combine the mixture with your hands. Scoop the meatloaf mixture and stuff it into muffin tins. Fill them ¾ full. Place in the oven and bake for 25 minutes until the top is lightly brown.

Cook the tomatoes in the pan until the skin starts to blister. Add the chipotle pepper, salt and olive oil in the food processor. Blend until you have a nice consistency. Pour the sauce into a pan and simmer before adding the cilantro. Garnish with avocado, salt, relish and lime.

Nutrient Information: 210 calories, 14 g fat, 3 g net carbs, 16.7 g protein

Almond Pumpkin Breakfast Bread

Ingredients:

- 1 ½ cups almond flour

- ½ cup coconut flour

- 5 tsp. pumpkin pie spice

- 1 ½ tsp. baking soda

- 1 ½ tsp. baking powder

- 1 tsp. sea salt

- 1 can (15 oz.) pumpkin puree (NOT pie filling)

- 4 eggs

- ½ cup maple syrup

- 5 tbsp. melted coconut oil

- 2 tsp. vanilla extract

Directions:

Begin by pre-heating your oven to 350 degrees. While your oven pre-heats, line a loaf pan with parchment paper.

Now, take a mixing bowl and combine your coconut flour, almond flour, baking soda, pumpkin pie spice, baking powder, and salt. Mix together well using a whisk or your hands.

Now, take another bowl and combine your eggs, pumpkin puree, coconut oil, maple syrup, and vanilla extract. Whisk these ingredients together until blended well and then add in your dry ingredient mixture and whisk together until smooth.

Pour your smooth batter in to your lined loaf pan and then bake in your pre-heated oven for an hour or until cooked through. Allow to cool to warm before eating.

Nutrition Information: 248 calories, 12.1g fat, 28.3g carbs, 5.8g protein

Protein Breakfast Bars

Ingredients:

- 2 cups walnuts

- 1 cup pecans

- 2 cups almonds

- 1 cup pumpkin seeds

- 1 cup dry cranberries

- 1 cup vanilla protein powder of your choice

- ½ cup pitted dates

- ½ cup raisins

- ½ cup coconut flour

- ¼ cup maple syrup

- 3 tbsp. coconut oil

- 1 tbsp. vanilla extract

- 1 ½ tsp. cinnamon

- 1 ½ tsp. molasses

Directions:

Begin by pre-heating your oven 220 degrees. As your oven is heating, line a baking tray and spread out your pecans and walnuts so that you can bake them.

Once your oven us pre-heated, roast the nuts for 30 minutes until they are fragrant. Remove the nuts from the oven and set aside.

Increase your oven temperature to 230 degrees. As your oven pre-heats again, take a 9" x 13" pan and grease it using coconut butter.

In your blender, combine your pecans, walnuts and your almonds together and pulse until you get a small gravel-like consistency.

Pour this nut mixture in to a mixing bowl and then add in your cranberries, pumpkin seeds, dates, protein powder, raisins, maple syrup, coconut flour, vanilla extract, coconut oil, molasses and cinnamon. Use a silicone spatula to mix these ingredients together well.

Once mixed, scoop these ingredients in to your greased pan. Put your pan in your pre-heated oven and cook for 40 minutes or until browned.

Nutrition Information: 356 calories, 22g fat, 25.3g carbs, 12.5g protein

Paleo Banana Pudding

Ingredients:

1 cup unsweetened almond milk

1 ripe banana

1 Tbsp. flax seed

1/2 tsp. vanilla

1 Tbsp. coffee

Directions:

1.   Simply place all ingredients in the blender.

2.   Activate until texture is smooth.

3.   Refrigerate a few hours before serving in a dessert bowl, or fruit bowl.

Nutrition Information : 325 Cal, 13 g total fat ,50 g carb., 15g protein.

Paleo Leeks Mushroom Quiche

Ingredients:

10 large eggs

1 cup chopped leeks (green and white parts)

1 cup sliced mushrooms

2 minced garlic cloves

1.5 cups coconut milk

1 Tbsp. Baking powder

Salt and pepper to taste

Directions:

1.   Preheat oven to 350 F.

2.   In a bowl mix in the eggs, coconut milk first. Add the other ingredients: mushrooms, leeks, garlic, salt and pepper.   Save a few green chopped leeks to decorate when serving.

3.   Bake the quiche for about 40 minutes.

Nutrition Information per serving: 195 Cal, 12 g total ,3.5 g carb,, 14g protein.

Energy Healthy Nuts Bars

Ingredients:

1 cup nuts (almond and pumpkins seeds)

3/4 cup pitted dates

3/4 cup other dried apricots

Pinch of salt

Directions:

1.   Simply place the cashews and pumpkin seeds in the food processer and activate until you are left with a mixture with large crumbs.

2.   Gradually Incorporate dates and dried apricots until the mixture becomes sticky.

3.   Place parchment paper in a square dish and press the mixture against the dish. Cover and refrigerate until serving.

4.   Keep in the refrigerator and enjoy

Nutrition Information : 198 Cal, 8 g total fat ,30 g carb, 4g protein.

Delight Casserole

Ingredients:

12 eggs

2 cup chopped yellow onion

1 minced clove garlic

1 cup chopped mixed yellow and red bell peppers

1 pound ground turkey

2 Tbsp. chili powder

Olive Oil

Salt and pepper

Optional: fresh guacamole when serving-

Directions:

Preheat oven at 375 F.

Prepare all the ingredients, chop the veggies and mince the garlic.

Cook the veggies in the olive oil for a few minutes in a skillet, and add the ground turkey.

In a bowl crack all the eggs, beat.

Add the egg mixture and also all the seasonings.

Pour the mixture into a previously greased baking dish.

Bake for approximately 40 minutes.

Nutrition Information per serving: 132 Cal, 7 g total fat , 3.2 g carb, 14g protein.

Vanilla Blueberry Scones

Ingredients:

1 egg

¼ cup melted Grass fed butter

¼ cup raw sugar

2 cups coconut flour

2 Tbsp. cornstarch

½ tsp. vanilla

1 ½ cup fresh blueberries

1 tsp. baking powder

Directions:

1.   Preheat oven at 350 F.

2.   In a bowl mix the egg, sugar, melted butter. Make sure it is mixed well; use the electric mixer if needed. Add the rest of ingredients, except the blueberries for now.

3.   Gently add the blueberries.

4.   Pour the batter into a greased round baking dish (if you don't have one, simply use a square one and instead of scones you will end up with squares)

5.   Bake for 350 F.

Nutrition Information: 160 Cal, 12 g total fat ,3.2 g carb,, 2g protein

Yummy Cauliflower Breakfast Hash

Ingredients:

1 lb Paleo chorizo

1 onion, chopped

2 garlic cloves, chopped

6 eggs

1 cauliflower head, riced

2 tomatoes, chopped

1 cup green onions

½ cup bell peppers

Spices of choice

Oil for frying

Directions:

Cook the chorizo in a large pan until it is brown. Add in the onions. Stir and cook. Add the garlic and cook for a minute.

Add the tomatoes and cauliflower. Fry the mixture for 7 minutes until the rice is cooked and tender.

Taste it and adjust the spices if needed.

Fry the eggs sunny side up and place on top of your chorizo. Spread the green onions on top then serve.

Nutrition facts: 274 calories, 12 g fat, 10 g net carbs, 30 g protein

Thyme Egg & Bacon Muffins

Ingredients:

8 Eggs

2/3 cup chopped red bell pepper

2 chopped green onions

½ cup crumbled bacon

1 tsp. thyme

A pinch of pepper

Directions:

1.   Preheat oven to 350 degrees

2.   Grease 8 muffins cups with coconut oil.

3.   Wisk together the eggs, bacon, pepper, green onion, thyme and pepper.

4.   Pour the eggs mixture in each muffin cup and bake for 20 minutes or so.

Nutrition Information per serving: 255 Cal, 3.5 g total fat , 6.5 g carb., 21g protein.

Sunday Vegetable Frittata

Ingredients:

5 eggs, separated

4 small or medium Yukon potatoes, sliced

2 small leeks, chopped

1 cup kale, chopped

½ tsp salt

½ tsp black pepper

3 tbsp coconut oil

8 egg whites

2 cloves garlic, minced

1 cup tomatoes, chopped

1 tbsp fresh basil

½ cup shredded cheese

Directions:

Set the oven at 350 degrees. Add one tablespoon of oil in a pan. Place over medium heat then cook the potatoes one layer at a time. Add more oil if you need to. Cook until it is golden brown. Place on top of a plate lined with paper towel. Add the kale, leek and garlic. Cook for 3 minutes then mix in the tomatoes. Cook for 2 minutes. Remove from heat then set aside. Leave the pan on top of the stove and reduce the heat.

Beat the egg white in a bowl using a mixer until fluffy. Add the egg yolks and whisk for 15 seconds. Place the potatoes on the pan. Layer it carefully to form the crust. Bake for 20 minutes. Turn the broiler for 5 minute and cook until brown.

Nutrient facts: 267 calories, 13 g fat, 21 g net carbs, 15.5 g protein

Chapter 6 PALEO LUNCH RECIPES

Onion Chicken with Habanero

Ingredients

- 2 ½ pounds chicken breast
- Pepper and salt
- 1/3 cup vinegar
- 1 cup diced tomatoes
- 2 tablespoons orange juice
- 1 teaspoon orange zest
- 2 cloves minced garlic
- 1 chopped onion
- 2 tablespoons achiote paste
- 1 tablespoon habanero sauce

Directions

1. Mix all the ingredients and cover the chicken with it.
2. Refrigerate for at least an hour or leave overnight if possible.
3. Heat up vegetable oil and fry the chicken until it is cooked.
4. Serve hot

Nutrition Information: 345 calories, 8.2g fat, 4.5g carbs, 52.5g protein

Leftover Beef Marinade

Ingredients

- 1 pound cooked and chopped beef
- 1 teaspoon dried thyme
- 1 teaspoon dried rosemary
- 1 minced garlic clove
- ½ chopped onion
- ¼ teaspoon mustard powder
- ¼ teaspoon pepper
- ½ teaspoon salt
- 1 tablespoon Worcestershire
- 1 tablespoon honey
- 1 cup vinegar
- 3 tablespoons tomato paste

Directions

1. HEAT ALL THE INGREDIENTS EXCEPT THE BEEF FOR TEN MINUTES.

2. NOW ADD THE BEEF AND SIMMER FOR FURTHER TEN MINUTES.

3. Serve hot with a serving of mashed potatoes and steamed or stir-fry veggies.

Nutrition Information: 262 calories,7.3g fat, 3.5g carbs, 35.2g protein

Delicious Tilapia Pesto Fillets

Ingredients:

- Pepper and salt to taste
- Cooking spray
- 2 tablespoons almond flour
- 2 tablespoons pesto sauce
- 6 Tilapia fillets
- Grated ginger (optional)
- Fennel seeds (optIonal)

Directions

1. Start off by preheating oven to 400F

2. Grease a baking pan with cooking spray

3. Take each fillet and line in the greased pan. Now place the other ingredients on top.

4. Alternately you can put all the ingredients in a plastic bag and shake to evenly coat the fillets.

5. Bake the fillets for ten minutes, or until firm.

6. Serve with any favorite veggie side.

Nutrition Information: 169calories,7.9g fat, 3.5g carbs, 23.5g protein

Vegetables Fish in Curry

Ingredients

- 1 pound white fish fillets
- 1 can coconut milk (unsweetened)
- 1 tablespoon red curry paste
- 2 medium carrots (sliced into small strips)
- ½ small cabbage
- ¼ cup cilantro leaves (finely chopped)

Directions

1. Cut white fish fillets into 1-inch pieces.

2. Cook coconut milk over medium heat in a large pan for 3 minutes and as you stir, add vegetables except the cilantro.

3. Cook and then cover for 5 minutes until the carrots get cooked.

4. Place the fish fillets into it and again cook for 5 minutes.

5. Top this dish with cilantro and serve.

Nutrition Information: 205 calories,7g fat, 20g carbs, 29g protein

Avocado Chicken Cups

Ingredients:

1 tbsp coconut oil

¼ cup orange juice

½ tsp oregano leaves, dried

½ onion, finely chopped

1 mango, chopped into bite size

1 tbsp lime juice

3 garlic cloves, minced

¼ cup lemon Juice

½ lb chicken, shredded or chopped

2 avocados, medium, cut in half with the pits removed

¼ cup cilantro leaves, chopped

½ tsp salt

Directions:

Add the oil to the pan and cook the garlic. Stir and cook until it is soft and translucent. Pour the lemon juice to the pan. To make the sauce, add the oregano leaves. Increase the heat and bring to a simmer. Pour the mojo in a bowl and set it aside.

Add ½ tbsp oil in a pan (the rest would be used later). Cook the shredded chicken until done. Add the sliced onion and 4 tablespoon mojo sauce. Toss the mixture to coat. Reduce the heat and cook for another 6 minutes until the onions become soft. Pour the remaining sauce then remove from the heat.

Cut the skin from the avocado's rounded end to prevent it from rolling when placed on plates. Place the chicken on top and add the mango, lime, salt, and cilantro. Serve.

Nutrient facts: 454 calories, 33 g fat, 8 g net carbs, 25 g protein

Ginger Braised Pork Shank

Ingredients:

4 lb pork shank

4 apples

½ head Napa cabbage

1 bay leaf

1 tsp ginger, grated

1 whole mace avril

1 orange zest

1 large onion

3 tbsp coconut oil

1 cup white wine

½ tsp whole cloves

1 stick cinnamon

Directions:

Set your oven at 300 degrees. Peel and remove the core of the apple. Chop each apple to 8-10 pieces. Cut the onion into large wedges. Chop the Napa cabbage. Heat the oil in a Dutch oven over medium heat. Cook the shank in several batches. Cook for 3 minutes at each side. Add more lard if desired.

Add onion to your pot and cook until it is brown. Mix in the cabbage, apple, orange zest, juice, wine and spices to the pot. Stir then add the shanks. Bake in the oven for 3 hours.

Make the gravy. Set the shanks aside and discard the bay leaf, mace and cinnamon. Blend the mixture until smooth. You can simmer the mixture to make it thicker. Serve with the meat.

Nutrient facts: 411 calories, 23 g fat, 16 g net carbs, 29 g protein

Herbs Grilled Chicken

Ingredients

- 2 ½ pounds chicken breast
- 1 bay leaf
- 1/3 cup vegetable oil
- 3 tablespoons vinegar
- 2 minced garlic cloves
- 4 tablespoons chopped parsley
- ¼ teaspoon salt
- 1 tablespoon fresh ground pepper
- ¼ cup chopped spring onions
- ¼ cup chopped oregano
- 4 tablespoons chopped rosemary

Directions

1. Mix herbs, pepper and salt in a bag the add chicken and shake well to cover.

2. Keep chicken in the marinade in a refrigerator for at least an hour.

3. Turn oven on to grill and cook the chicken.

4. Serve with some gravy and favorite vegetables.

5. Optionally, grass-fed beef can be used in place of chicken.

Nutrition Information: 520 calories,27g fat, 20g carbs, 29g protein

Pecan Crust Chicken

Ingredients:

2 Tbsp. honey (raw, organic)

½ c. mustard (Dijon)

4 chicken breasts (skinless, boneless, whole)

1 c. pecans (crushed)

Directions:

1. Preheat the oven to 350 degrees. Whisk the honey and mustard in a medium size bowl.

2. Use a food processor to chop the pecans to a very fine texture. Place them in a large-sized bowl.

3. Remove all of the extra juice from the chicken breasts with paper towels.

4. Take one chicken breast and place it in the honey mustard mix. Make sure both sides are covered completely. Place it in the bowl with the pecan mixture. Coat both sides evenly. Repeat this process for the remaining chicken breast. You can also add a little sea salt to each if you desire.

5. Place them in a glass dish for baking and let them bake for about 45 minutes.

Nutritional Information: Calories 600, Carbs 17 g, Fat 37 g, Protein 54 g

Vietnamese Stir Fry

Ingredients:

Walnut oil (for cooking)

2 garlic cloves (minced)

½ red bell pepper (chopped)

1 tsp. ginger (grated)

1 carrot (peeled, shredded)

2 c. chicken (precooked chopped)

1 zucchini (spiral sliced into noodles)

2 ½ tsp. curry powder

1 tsp. fish sauce

1 ½ tsp. sesame oil (toasted)

Black pepper (as desired)

Coriander (as needed, fresh, chopped)

1 lime (for juice)

Directions:

1. Use a medium-sized saucepan to warm the walnut oil on medium heat.

2. Toss in the garlic, red bell pepper, and ginger. Let this simmer for a few minutes then toss in the carrots. Continue simmer about 2 more minutes.

3. Toss in the meat and cook so that it is warmed. Turn the heat up to medium-high and add the zucchini noodles. Sprinkle the curry powder and keep stirring it as you add the fish sauce, sesame oil, black pepper, coriander, and lime juice.

4. Make sure the pan is constantly moving as you cook the stir fry. Keep cooking the mixture until the zucchini noodles are starting to become clear.

5. Divide the mixture up between two serving bowls and sprinkle a little coriander on top. Serve.

Nutritional Information: Calories 140, Carbs 10 g, Fat 9 g, Protein 6 g

Delight Savory Salmon Cakes

Ingredients:

1 6oz. can of salmon (skinless, boneless)

1 celery rib (diced)

1 tsp. lemon pepper

1 Tbsp. dill (dried)

¼ tsp. sea salt

½ onion (medium, peel removed, diced)

1 ½ Tbsp. flour (coconut)

2 eggs (large)

3 Tbsp. coconut oil

Directions:

1. Place the salmon in a large-sized bowl and break it up using a fork. Toss in the celery, lemon pepper, dill, sea salt, and onion. Add the coconut flour and mix together.

2. Toss the eggs in next and stir for about 1 minute.

3. Warm the coconut oil in a large-sized skillet over medium-high heat.

4. Take the salmon mixture and form it into 5, two inch wide, patties. Place the patties in the skillet and let them cook for about 4 minutes on each side. They should be golden in color when they are ready.

Nutritional Informations: Calories 150, Carbs .2 g, Fat 13 g, Protein 10 g

Garlic Creamy Celery Soup

Ingredients:

2 cloves of garlic (chopped)

2 sprigs of thyme

½ onion (yellow, chopped)

4 c. chicken bone broth

2 celery roots (large, peeled, cut into ½ inch cubes)

½ c. white wine (dry)

2 Tbsp. butter

Directions:

1. Use a large-sized pot or a stock pot. Put the garlic, thyme, onion, chicken broth, and celery root into the pot. Let it boil for a few minutes. Lower the heat and let it simmer for about 25 minutes. Celery root should be soft.

2. Pour the soup into a blender and set it to puree. Pour it back into the pot and add the wine and butter. Let it simmer for about 5 minutes.

3. Serve!

Nutritional Informations: Calories 160, Carbs 12 g, Fat 3 g, Protein 14 g

Chicken Sun-dried Tomatoes Dish

Ingredients:

2 Tbsp. olive oil

5 oz. spinach (baby)

Pepper (as desired)

½ c. tomatoes (sun-dried, chopped)

2 cloves of garlic (minced)

Salt (as desired)

2 c. chicken (organic, cooked, shredded)

3 bell peppers (cut in half)

Directions:

1. Preheat oven to 350 degrees. Grease a baking sheet.

2. Warm 2 tablespoons of olive oil on medium-low heat, in a large-sized skillet. Toss in the spinach and let it cook until it becomes limp. Toss in the pepper, sun-dried tomatoes, garlic, and salt. Cook for about 2 minutes.

3. Toss in chicken and stir. Make sure everything has warmed through before placing the mixture inside the bell peppers. Place the peppers on the pan and cover the pan with foil.

4. Bake for about 30 minutes.

Nutritional Informations: Calories 270, Carbs 13 g, Fat 12 g, Protein 29 g

Pomegranate Glazed Salmon

Ingredients:

4 salmon fillets

4 garlic cloves, crushed

2 tbsp pomegranate molasses

1 tbsp ginger, grated

¼ cup orange juice

1 tbsp coconut oil

Directions:

Mix the orange juice, ginger and garlic in a bowl. Add 2 tablespoon of the molasses and pour it over the salmon. Let it marinate for 15 minutes. Set the oven at 425 degrees.

Cover the baking sheet with foil. Grease it with coconut oil. You can skip this step if your salmon has skin.

Place the fish on the baking sheet then spread more molasses on each salmon. Bake for 12-15 minutes until it looks opaque.

Nutrient facts: 310 calories, 14.5 g fat, 11 g net carbs, 35 g protein

Delicious Drumsticks

Ingredients:

- 6 drumsticks
- 2 minced garlic cloves
- 1 tablespoon vinegar
- 1/2 cup chipotle peppers in adobo sauce
- 1/2 cup water
- 1 teaspoon salt

Directions:

1. Use a blender to mix peppers in sauce with water.

2. Rub over chicken and refrigerate it for 1-12 hours.

3. Preheat oven to 400F and bake in a covered dish for about 45 minutes, or until cooked.

4. Finish cooking under the grill.

5. Optionally, steaks can be used in place of chicken and peppers can be replaced with any favorite sauce.

Nutrition Information: 210 calories,9g fat, 12g carbs,30g protein

Paleo Meatballs Spaghetti

Ingredients:

3 lb summer squash

16 garlic cloves, minced

1 ½ cups whole black olive

¾ cup basil, chopped

1 tbsp salt

10 oz mushrooms, sliced

5 slices bacon

For the meatballs:

¼ tsp salt

2 lb ground beef

¼ cup oregano, chopped

Directions:

Use a vegetable spiraler to cut your squash into noodles. Place in a strainer and season it with salt. Let it sit for an hour. Rinse though with water. Let the noodles drain and set it on top of paper towels to absorb the water.

Chop the bacon into small pieces. Place a large pan or pot over medium heat. Cook the bacon until it is brown. Mix in the garlic and mushrooms. Continue to cook for 8 minutes until the mushrooms are soft and brown. Add the squash noodles and olives. Toss and stir for 5 minutes until it is cooked. Add the basil and stir for a few seconds. Add the meatballs and serve.

Nutrient facts: 280 calories, 12.6 g fat, 11 g net carbs, 51 g protein

Yummy Beef Jerky Apple Mix

Ingredients:

1 tsp. crushed red pepper

1 apple (small, core removed, sliced)

1 oz. Beef jerky (all natural)

Directions:

1. Sprinkle the red pepper on the slices of apple.

2. Serve the apples with the beef jerky.

Nutritional Informations: Calories 196, Carbs 24 g, Fat 8 g, Protein 10 g

Japanese Noodle Soup

Ingredients:

2 pieces kombu kelp

4 cups water

1 lb kelp noodles

1 tbsp coconut water vinegar

1 cup lightly packed bonito flakes

2 tilapia or cod

2 tbsp coconut aminos

4 cups loosely packed greens

Directions:

Place the bonito and kombu in a large pot and add water. Bring to a boil then reduce the temperature and simmer for 10 minutes.

Chop the greens and place in a bowl. Cut fish into cubes. Rinse the kelp in running water. Strain the broth using a cheese cloth to remove the kombu and bonito.

Return the broth to the pot. Mix in the coconut vinegar and coconut aminos. Add the fish to the pot and cook until done. If you are using tough greens like snow peas, cabbage and bok choy, add it at the same time as the fish but if you are using tender greens like chard and spinach add them after the fish is cooked.

Mix in the kelp noodles. Simmer for 3 minutes before serving.

Nutrient facts: 105 calories, 0.7 g fat, 1.3 g net carbs, 18 g protein

Healthy Fried Rice

Ingredients:

Olive oil

1 head of cauliflower (small, grated)

Garlic (as desired, chopped)

Onions (as desired, chopped)

Celery (as desired, chopped)

Cabbage (as desired, chopped)

Mushrooms (as desired, chopped)

Scallions (as desired, chopped for garnish)

1 Tbsp. soy sauce

1 egg

Pepper (as desired)

Salt (as desired)

Directions:

1. Use a food processor to grate the cauliflower.

2. Warm the olive oil on medium heat, in a large-sized pan.

3. Toss in the garlic and onions and cook until they become clear. Add in the celery, cabbage and mushrooms. Pour in the soy sauce and stir. Let this cook for a few minutes.

4. Add the cauliflower in and mix everything together. Let this cook for about 4 minutes. Move everything away from the center of the mixture and pour in the egg. Mix and let this cook a few more minutes. Sprinkle with pepper and salt. Garnish with scallions.

5. Serve!

Nutritional Informations: Calories 90, Carbs 9 g, Fat 5 g, Protein 3 g

Mexican Pork

Ingredients:

3 lbs. pork shoulder (cooked, shredded)

1 8oz.can tomato sauce

1 Tbsp. chili powder

1 tsp. red pepper (crushed)

2 tsp. cayenne pepper

½ tsp. nutmeg

½ tsp. paprika

Pepper (as desired)

¼ tsp. cloves (ground)

1 7oz. can of green chilies

Salt (as desired)

Avocados (as needed)

Directions:

1. Grease a saucepan and warm it over medium heat. On medium heat, cook the pork and tomato sauce. Add the chili powder, red pepper, cayenne pepper, nutmeg, paprika, pepper, cloves, green chilies, and salt. Stir.

2. Turn the heat down to low and let it simmer for 20 minutes. Do not stir.

3. Place on a serving plate and add fresh avocados as garnish.

Nutritional Informations: Calories 580, Carbs 12 g, Fat 27 g, Protein 71 g

Delicious Chicken Salad

Ingredients:

- 2 chopped celery stalks
- 2 chopped fully cooked chicken breasts
- ½ cup dried cranberries
- ½ cup chopped pecans
- ⅓ cup Paleo Mayo
- 1 tablespoon honey
- 1 teaspoon poppy seeds
- 1 tablespoon apple cider vinegar

Directions

1. Put all the ingredients in a bowl and toss.

Nutrition Information: 290 calories,12g fat, 12g carbs, 28g protein

Lemon Salmon Salad

Ingredients:

- 1 lb. salmon fillet
- 2 t capers (drained and rinsed)
- 1 stalk chopped celery
- Juice and zest from 1/2 lemon
- Drizzle of extra virgin olive oil
- 1 tsp. fresh dill
- Sea salt and pepper to taste

Directions

1. Season salmon fillet with salt and pepper and bake at 350 until it becomes opaque (5-10 minutes). Let them to cool and flake salmon. (It should flake easily)

2. Add all the remaining ingredients.

Nutrition Information: 220calories,6g fat, 8g carbs, 22g protein

Healthy Thai Chicken Wraps

Ingredients:

Filling:

- 1 lb. grilled (boneless and skinless) chicken breast - diced into ½ " cubes

- 1 shredded carrot

- 3 green onions (thinly sliced)

- 4 thinly chopped Napa cabbages leaves

- 1 cup chopped broccoli (raw)

- 12 Bib or Romaine lettuce leaves

- Cilantro

- ¼ cup water

Thai Sauce:

- ¼ cup almond butter

- 2 garlic cloves minced

- 2 tablespoons coconut aminos (gives soy sauce flavor)

- 2 tablespoons lime juice

Directions:

1.   Grill and cut up the chicken and add the remaining ingredients except the lettuce leaves.

2.   Spoon chicken mixture into the lettuce leaves and drizzle Thai sauce over it. Chicken mixture and Thai sauce can be made ahead.

3.   Leave in refrigerator and spoon into the romaine or Bibb lettuce leaf.

Nutrition Information: 385 calories,12g fat, 22g carbs, 45g protein

Fresh Baked Salmon

Ingredients:

2 salmon fillets (Alaskan, wild caught)

¼ c. walnut oil

¼ tsp. dill weed

¼ tsp. salt

¼ tsp. garlic powder

¼ tsp. pepper

¼ tsp. red pepper flakes

Directions:

1. Preheat the oven to 450 degrees.

2. Lay the fillets in a baking dish that is glass.

3. Pour the walnut oil on the fillets and then sprinkle on the dill, salt, garlic, pepper, and red pepper.

4. Let the fillets bake for about 20 minutes.

5. Serve.

Nutritional Informations: Calories 240, Carbs 0 g, Fat 21 g, Protein 11 g

Simple Paleo Guacamole

Ingredients:

2 avocados (ripe, peeled, pits removed)

1 lime (for juice)

Black pepper (as desired)

1 jalapeno pepper (diced)

1 tomato (Roma, seeds removed, diced)

1 garlic clove (minced)

Salt (as desired)

1/2 onion (small, minced)

1 Tbsp. Cilantro (fresh, chopped)

Directions:

1. In a large-sized bowl, add the avocados and pour the lime juice right on top.

2. Use a fork to mash it completely. Toss in the pepper, jalapeno pepper, tomato, garlic, salt, onion, and cilantro.

Nutritional Informations: Calories 118, Carbs 8 g, Fat 10 g, Protein 2 g

Crispy Salsa Taco Salad

Ingredients:

2 tsp. garlic powder

2 Tbsp. chili powder

2 tsp. cumin (ground)

Salt (as needed)

½ tsp. cayenne pepper

Black pepper (as needed)

1 lb. beef (ground)

2 garlic cloves (minced)

1 onion (diced)

½ c. salsa

¼ c. sour cream

1 Tbsp. lime juice

2 romaine hearts (shredded)

3 c. tomatoes (cherry, cut in half)

¼ c. cheddar cheese (shredded)

1/3 c. cilantro (chopped)

Directions:

1. In a small-sized bowl, mix the garlic powder, chili powder, cumin, salt, cayenne pepper, and black pepper.

2. Cook the beef in a large-sized skillet on medium-high heat, for about 10 minutes. Make sure it has completely browned. Toss in the garlic and onion. Continue stirring and cooking for 5 more minutes. Add the spices. Mix and cook for an additional 3 minutes.

3. In a small-sized bowl, mix the lime juice, salsa, and sour cream. Place an even amount of lettuce on a large serving plate. Add some of meat mixture, then some salsa mixture. Top with cilantro, tomatoes, and cheese, if desired.

Nutritional Informations: Calories 385, Carbs 19 g, Fat 25 g, Protein 25 g

Chicken Vegetable Soup

Ingredients:

- 3 cups of chicken stock
- 2 cups of your favorite vegetables chopped or sliced
- 6 ounces left over chicken

Directions:

1.   Bring stock and then reduce and simmer for about five minutes.

2.   Stir in leftover chicken and vegetables of choice. Add 1 cup coconut milk, fresh ginger, and 2 tablespoons of fish sauce to create Asian flavors.

3.   To create Italian flavor, add one cup of fresh chopped tomato and fresh basil. To give Spanish flavor, add some fresh jalapeno or Serrano peppers.

Nutrition Information: 183 calories,13g fat, 22g carbs, 23g protein

Maple Syrup Chicken Burgers

Ingredients:

2 ½ lb ground chicken or turkey

1 large apple

2 tsp rosemary, chopped

8 oz bacon

1 onion

½ tsp salt

For the sauce:

½ cup maple syrup

2 cups frozen cranberries

¼ cup water

Directions:

Place the bacon in the pan and cook until it is crispy. Dice the onion and apple. Chop the rosemary. Remove the bacon from the pan and add the fat and onion. Cook for 5 minutes until the onions are soft. Add the rosemary and apple. Continue to cook until it is done.

Chop the bacon into slices. Combine the chicken, onion mix, apple and bacon. Mix with your hands and form into patties. Add fat to a pan and cook the patties. Flip once and cook for one minute.

Make the sauce. Combine the ingredients in a saucepan and boil. Simmer for 10 minutes and stir occasionally. Serve with the burgers.

Nutrient facts: 406 calories, 18 g fat, 15 g net carbs, 42 g protein

Yummy Lamb Meatballs

Ingredients:

- ¼ teaspoon cinnamon
- ¼ teaspoon black pepper
- ½ teaspoon ground cumin
- ½ onion, chopped
- 1 teaspoon ground coriander
- 1 teaspoon salt
- 1 egg
- 1 tablespoon chopped fresh mint
- 1 tablespoon chopped fresh cilantro
- 1 pound minced lamb
- 2 garlic cloves, minced
- Sesame seeds (optional)

Directions

1. Begin by preheating your oven to 375F.

2. In a bowl mix all the ingredients together thoroughly.

3. Use your hands to shape the mixture into small meatballs.

4. Grease a baking dish with cooking oil and bake the meatballs for ten minutes

5. After a while turn them over and cook for further 5-10 minutes, until thoroughly cooked.

Nutrition Information: 189 calories,7.6g fat, 15g carbs, 26.9g protein

Honey Mustard Cobb Salad

Ingredients:

- 3 cups mixed lettuce leaves (chopped)

- 3 eggs cut into quarters (hard boiled)

- 1 cup chicken breast (cooked and then diced)

- 1 tomato (diced)

- ½ cup crispy bacon bits (crumbled)

- ½ onion (diced)

- ½ cucumber (diced)

- ½ cup blue cheese (crumbled)

For dressing:

- 2 teaspoons honey

- 2 teaspoons mustard (wholegrain)

- 1 garlic clove (minced)

- 1 tablespoon parsley (finely chopped)

- Salt and pepper to taste

Directions

1. In a bowl, first place the mixed lettuce leaves in order to make a base.

2. Then arrange the other salad ingredients in lines on the lettuce.

3. Mix the dressing ingredients and whisk and drizzle over the salad.

4. Optionally, a mix of chopped nuts can be added over it for some crunch.

Steak with Red Wine Sauce

Nutrition Information: 400 calories,20g fat, 15g carbs, 22g protein

Garlic sirloin fillet steak

Ingredients:

- 1 pound sirloin fillet steak
- ½ cup red wine (good quality)
- Plenty of grass fed butter
- 1 teaspoon fresh parsley (chopped)
- 2 garlic cloves (crushed)
- Salt to taste
- black pepper to taste (freshly ground)

Directions

1. Season the meat on both sides. Heat the butter in a big skillet. Put the fillet in the hot pan and sear for 3 - 4 minutes or until brown.

2. Immediately remove and cover the steak in foil. In this way we can prevent the meat becoming tough or cold and it will keep cooking further.

3. In the pan, as we have hot browned butter and the juices from the steak. Add the garlic and cook until fragrant, but do not brown.

4. Add wine and rapidly boil off the alcohol on high heat with continuous stirring for a few minutes to get a sticky reduction that we can pour over the sliced steak.

Nutrition Information: 300 calories,12g fat, 15g carbs, 55g protein

Yogurt Sauce Lamb Kofta

Ingredients

- 1 pound lamb (minced)
- ½ onion (grated)
- 1 teaspoon salt
- 1 teaspoon cumin (ground)
- 4 garlic cloves (finely minced)
- 6 – 8 wooden skewers
- 1 tablespoon coriander (ground)
- ¼ teaspoon black pepper (ground)
- ½ teaspoon cinnamon
- ¼ teaspoon cayenne pepper
- 3 tablespoons fresh parsley (chopped)
- ½ teaspoon allspice (ground)
- ¼ teaspoon ginger (ground)

To make the mint sauce:

- 3 tablespoons fresh mint leaves (finely minced)
- 2 garlic cloves (finely minced)
- ½ cucumber (grated)
- ½ cup thick Greek yogurt
- 2 teaspoons lemon juice
- Salt and pepper to taste

Directions

1. Mix all the ingredients in a bowl by hand.

2.   Soak the skewers in water for 30 minutes to prevent burning.

3.   Pick a small handful of the lamb mixture and build it around the skewers to give it the shape of a sausage. Prepare as many as possible.

4.   The koftas / kebabs can be baked in an oven preheated at 180 degrees Celsius or it can be grilled on a barbecue.

5.   Mix all the ingredients well for the yogurt and mint sauce and serve with koftas / kebabs.

Nutrition Information: 248 calories,22g fat, 12g carbs, 30g protein

Spicy Grilled Shrimp

Ingredients:

- 1 ½ lbs. medium shrimp (deveined and peeled)
- 1 tablespoon garlic (minced)
- ¼ cup lemon juice
- ¼ cup olive oil
- Crushed red pepper flakes to taste
- Ground black pepper to taste
- 3 tablespoons fresh parsley (chopped)

Directions

1.   In a non-reactive bowl, mix olive oil, garlic and black pepper. Add shrimp and toss all the ingredients to coat it and add the red pepper flakes to taste and then put it in a bowl.

2.   Put the bowl in a fridge for 30 minutes to marinate.

3.   Preheat the grill to high heat. Lightly oil the grill, grill shrimp for about two minutes on each side to make opaque.

Nutrition Information: 210 calories, 14g fat, 10g carbs, 20g protein

Delicious Spicy Roasted Chicken

Ingredients

- 3 lb. whole chicken
- 1 tablespoon olive oil
- 1 teaspoon salt
- ¼ teaspoon basil
- ¼ teaspoon oregano
- ¼ teaspoon black pepper (ground)
- ¼ teaspoon paprika
- ⅛ teaspoon cayenne pepper

Directions

1.   Rinse whole chicken properly under cold water to remove access fat. Pat dry the chicken using a paper towel.

2.   Preheat oven to 450F. Place chicken in a pan and rub with olive oil. Add basil, paprika, oregano, black pepper, salt and cayenne pepper to chicken. Roast the chicken for about 20 minutes and then lower heat to 400F. Keep

roasting for about 40 minutes so that the internal temperature is about 165 F. Allow to cool for 10-15 minutes.

Nutrition Information: 412 calories, 13g fat, 12g carbs, 43g protein

Mouth Watering Salmon Salad

Ingredients:

- salmon ribbons (smoked)
- 3 eggs (hard boiled)
- 1 bunch of rocket leaves
- 3 - 4 green onions (chopped)
- 1/3 cup cream cheese
- 1 tablespoon capers
- 1 tablespoon lemon juice
- 1 tablespoon fresh parsley (chopped)
- I cucumber (cut into chunky wedges)
- Salt and pepper to taste

Directions

1.   To create a dressing, combine the lemon juice, cream cheese, salt and pepper together and whisk properly.

2.   Prepare a base of the rocket leaves and then make a layer of the salmon ribbons, onions, cucumber, parsley and the hard boiled eggs on it.

3.   Use cream cheese as dressing and sprinkle capers over it.

Nutrition Information: 205 calories, 12g fat, 15g carbs, 18g protein

Mushroom with Stir Fry Napa Cabbage

Ingredients:

½ c. bacon (diced)

1 onion (small, sliced thin)

8 oz. mushrooms (cremini, sliced thin)

¼ c. chicken broth

1 head of napa cabbage (small, cut into ½" strips)

Directions:

1. Cook the bacon on medium heat in a large-sized cast iron pan.

2. Toss in the onions and let them cook until they start to look clear. Add the mushrooms in and let them simmer for a few minutes.

3. Add the chicken broth and cabbage and stir. Cover and let this cook for about 10 minutes. The cabbage should be soft. Sprinkle with pepper and salt as desired and serve.

Nutritional Informations: Calories 160, Carbs 12 g, Fat 10 g, Protein 7 g

Tasty Curried Cabbage Stir Fry

Ingredients:

1 Tbsp. ghee

½ onion (large, diced)

1 lb. beef (ground)

Pepper (fresh, ground, as desired)

2 tsp. curry powder

Salt (Kosher, as desired)

½ head of cabbage (small, sliced thin)

½ lime (for juice)

Directions:

1. In a large-sized cast iron pan, warm the ghee and toss in the onions. Let them cook until they become clear. Toss in the beef. Break it apart as you let it cook. Make sure it has completely browned.

2. Add the pepper, curry powder, and salt. Stir.

3. Add the cabbage and cover. Let this cook for about 2 minutes. The cabbage should be fairly soft when it is done.

4. Squeeze in some lime juice.

5. Serve and enjoy!

Nutritional Informations :Calories 310, Carbs 11 g, Fat 20 g, Protein 23 g

Quick Paleo Style Chili

Ingredients:

2 garlic cloves

½ c. onion (minced)

½ c. green pepper (minced)

1 lb. beef (ground, lean)

8 oz. salsa

3 Tbsp. chili powder

1/8 tsp. flour (almond)

1 tsp. garlic powder

1 can of beef broth

1 large can of tomatoes (whole, no salt added, crush using your hand)

1 ½ Tbsp. cumin (ground)

Directions:

1. Toss the garlic, onion, and green pepper into a skillet. Add the beef and cook until it has browned.

2. Add in the salsa, chilli powder, almond flour, garlic powder, beef broth, tomatoes, and cumin.

3. Put chili in a crock pot and let it cook, on high, for about 4 hours.

Nutritional Informations: Calories 418, Carbs 14 g, Fat 16 g, Protein 51 g

Delight Buffalo Chicken Strips

Ingredients:

2 lb boneless and skinless chicken breast

½ cup water

2 tbsp dried oregano

2 tbsp ground cumin

½ cup cider vinegar

3 tbsp cayenne pepper

2 tbsp garlic powder

2 tbsp chili powder

Directions:

Cut the chicken into strips. Place the chicken in a sealable bag and mix in the water, pepper and vinegar.

Rub the spices into the chicken. Make sure that cayenne is distributed evenly. Set the oven at 350 degrees.

Place the chicken on the baking sheet. Sprinkle with the seasonings and bake for 20 minutes until done.

Nutrient facts: 2014 calories, 3.5 g fat, 4.3 g net carbs, 36 g protein

Turmeric Ginger Steak Salad

Ingredients:

2 tbsp coconut oil, divided

1 tsp turmeric, ground

1 tsp cumin seed, ground

4 cups baby spinach, washed and stems removed

420 g cauliflower, cut into florets

1 ½ lb beef flank, cut into portions

½ cup sweet and spicy tomato jam

Salt and pepper to taste

Directions:

Set your oven to 400 degrees.

Toss the cauliflower in a bowl of oil, turmeric, salt and pepper. Place the cauliflower in a baking sheet and roast for 12 minutes. Set the pan on top of medium heat.

Season the beef with pepper, cumin and salt. Add oil to the pan and cook the beef for 5 minutes on each side. Combine the spinach, tomato jam, salt and pepper.

Add the cauliflower to the bowl and toss to coat. Divide evenly into 4 plates. Slice the steak into strips and add to the salad.

Nutrient facts: 552 calories, 37 g fat, 8 g net carbs, 15 g protein

Bamboo Pork Chow Mein

Ingredients:

2 tbsp coconut oil

1 small onion, sliced in wedges

5 oz can bamboo shoots, sliced

8 baby mushrooms

1 cup bone broth

1 lb kelp noodles

1 lb pork loin chops, sliced thinly

5 oz can water chestnuts, sliced

4 dried shiitake mushrooms

3 baby bok choy

1 tbsp coconut vinegar

1 green onion

Directions:

Soak the dried mushrooms in water and set aside for half an hour. Rinse the mushrooms and slice it into thin strips. Slice the onion in wedges. Chop the mushrooms in quarters and separate the leaves of bok choy. Drain and rinse the chestnuts and bamboo shoots. Rinse the kelp noodles in flowing water.

Heat a large pan and add the coconut oil. Cook the pork and stir frequently until the meat is brown. Add the mushrooms, onion and bok choy. Slowly pour the coconut vinegar and broth. Cook and stir frequently for 10 minutes until the pork is done but the vegetables are al dente. Increase the heat. Create a hole in the middle by pushing the pork and vegetable to the sides. Place the kelp noodles in the middle and simmer for 3 minutes. Break the kelp noodles and spread it to the chow mein. Garnish with green onions before serving.

Nutrient facts: 488 calories, 29 g fat, 19 g net carbs, 34 g protein

Turkey Pumpkin chilli

Ingredients:

1 medium pumpkin, peeled and cut into cubes

2 tbsp coconut oil, melted

1 lb ground beef

8 celery stalks, chopped

3 bay laves

1 ½ tbsp cumin

1 tsp nutmeg

¼ tsp cayenne

1 ½ tbsp oregano, chopped

1 bunch fresh spinach, chopped

6 oz tomato paste

½ tsp salt to taste

1 large sweet potato, peeled and cubed

2 lb ground turkey

2 onions, chopped

8 garlic cloves, chopped

3 tbsp chili powder to taste

1 tsp cinnamon

2 tsp cocoa powder

1 ½ tbsp basil, chopped

2 tbsp cilantro, chopped

3 can diced tomatoes

2 cups pumpkin puree

Directions:

Combine the sweet potato and pumpkin in a bowl. Add the oil and toss to combine.

Spread it evenly in a baking pan and bake for 30 minutes at 350 degrees until it is brown and soft. Cook the beef and turkey in a pan. Add the bay leaves, onion, celery and garlic in a pot. Stir gently to avoid breaking the meat into very small pieces.

Add the cocoa, nutmeg, chili, cumin and cinnamon once the meat is cooked. Cook and stir until soft and fragrant.

Add the tomato paste, puree, tomatoes and salt. Simmer and reduce the heat. Simmer for 15 minutes until the celery is soft.

Garnish with spinach, oregano and basil. Add the sweet potato and pumpkin. Stir to combine.

Nutrient facts: 384 calories, 17 g fat, 15 g net carbs, 43 g protein

Flavors Grilled Iron Steak

Ingredients

- 2 flat iron steaks, 8 oz.
- ½ teaspoon onion powder
- ½ teaspoon garlic powder
- ½ teaspoon lemon pepper seasoning

Directions

1. Rub the dry seasoning over the steak covering both sides.

2. Wrap it up in plastic and set it in the fridge for an hour

3. Grill the steak at medium heat after leaving it at room temperature for a while.

Nutrition Information: 540 calories, 20g fat, 10g carbs, 69g protein

Chicken Wings Asian Style

Ingredients:

3 lb chicken wings, separated

4 garlic cloves, chopped

1 tsp anise seed

½ cup coconut aminos

2 tbsp coconut vinegar

2 tbsp sesame oil

2 tbsp coconut oil

1 tbsp ginger, chopped

1 tsp fennel seed

2 tbsp honey

1 tbsp fish sauce

Directions:

Place the chicken wings in a bowl. Heat the oil in a saucepan. Add the fennel, ginger, anise and garlic.

Stir until it is fragrant. Add the vinegar, honey, fish sauce and coconut aminos. Boil and simmer for one minute.

Add the sesame oil. Pour the mixture over the chicken wings and stir to coat. Marinate for 24 hours.

Drain and cook the wings in a grill. Turn once to cook the other side. You can also bake it for 45 minutes at 375 degrees.

Nutrient facts: 541 calories, 26 g fat, 8 g net carbohydrates, 66 g protein

Dill Parchment Salmon With Herb

Ingredients:

1 cup unsalted butter, softened

4 garlic cloves, crushed

1/3 cup parsley

¼ tsp ground pepper, to taste

1 lemon, zest

½ cup dill

½ tsp salt

4 8oz salmon fillet

Directions:

Mix the herbs and lemon zest in the food processor and blend until it is fine. Add the herb mixture to a bowl and stir to combine.

Set the oven at 350 degrees. Lay a sheet of tin foil on a baking sheet. The foil should be twice as long as the fish fillet.

Place the fish on the foil and make sure to leave enough space between the fish. Scoop the herb and spread it on top of the fillet.

Spread one tablespoon of water around the fish. Bake this for 20 minutes until the fish is opaque.

Nutrient facts: 668 calories, 57 g fat, 4.5 g net carbs, 36.7 g protein

Chapter 7 PALEO DINNER RECIPES

Almond Wrap Egg Smoked Salmon

Ingredients

- 4 slices smoked salmon
- 6 eggs
- ¼ cup radish, shredded
- 1 lemon, juiced
- ½ tsp. salt, pepper
- 4 almond wraps

Directions

1. Mix radish with lemon juice, set aside.

2. Whisk eggs with salt, pepper.

3. Heat 2 tbsp. extra virgin olive oil in nonstick pan.

4. Pour eggs into pan and cook a minute per side.

5. Divide omelet into four sections.

6. Place a quarter of omelet on almond wrap, top with smoked salmon and shredded radish and roll.

Nutrition Information: 217calories, 7g fat, 6g carbs, 27g protein

Tasty Mustard Gourmet Chicken

Ingredients:

- 1 lb. chicken breasts
- 3 tbsp. sardines, chopped
- 1 egg
- 1 tsp. dry mustard
- ½ lemon, juiced
- 2 cups green leaf lettuce, chopped
- ½ tsp. salt, black pepper
- Extra virgin olive oil

Directions

1. Preheat oven to 375 degrees and lightly coat glass baking dish with olive oil.

2. Combine sardines, egg, dry mustard, lemon juice, salt and pepper in food processor and mix until creamy.

3. Place chicken breasts in bottom of glass baking dish and pour creamy sauce over top.

4. Bake in oven for 20 minutes turning halfway.

5. Slice chicken breasts into strips, place on wrap alongside lettuce and wrap.

Nutrition Information: 246 calories, 107g fat, 0g carbs, 35g protein

Tasty Stuffed Cabbage Rolls

Ingredients:

1 head cabbage

1 pound ground pork

2 cloves

1 chopped onion

1 tsp. oregano salt and pepper

2 cups diced seasoned tomatoes

1 cup tomato sauce

Directions:

1.   Boil water in a large pot for cabbage. Remove the head and cook a few leaves at a time for a few minutes each.

2.   Meanwhile, mix the ground pork, seasonings, and veggies.

3.   When all leaves are cooked, fill with the ground pork mixture and place them in the slow cooker.

4.   Pour the tomatoes and tomato sauce on top.

5.   Cook for 6 or 7 hours in slow cooker at low temperature.

Nutrition Information per serving: 201 Cal, 9.6 g total 9.5 g carb, 21g protein

Fax Tortillas Avocado Shrimp

Ingredients:

- 1 lb. shrimp, peeled, deveined
- 1 red bell pepper, seeded and chopped
- 1 medium onion, peeled, chopped
- 1/2 avocado, pitted
- 1 lemon, juiced
- 1/2 tsp. salt, black pepper
- 4 flax tortillas

Directions:

1. Mix shrimp with bell pepper and onion in glass bowl.

2. Place avocado in blender and mix until smooth, add lemon juice, salt, pepper.

3. Mix avocado into shrimp mixture and place a quarter of mixture into each flax tortilla.

Nutrition Information: 145 calories, 8g fat, 0g carbs, 35g protein

Pork Bacon Wrapped

Ingredients:

4-5 pounds pork loin roast

2 tbsp. Olive oil

1 pound of turkey bacon

2 cups of pork or vegetable broth

1 Tsp. dried oregano

1 Tsp. dried thyme

1 Tbsp. dried sage

½ tsp basil

4 whole garlic cloves

1 chopped large yellow onion

1 can of unsweetened pineapple slices

Directions:

1. Preheat your own to 300 degrees F.

2. Prepare the pork by rubbing olive and garlic on it. Cover completely with uncooked bacon slices. Place on a baking dish.

3. In a bowl, mix the broth and all of the seasonings, then pour the mixture on the pork.

4. Place the garlic cloves and onion on the side.

5. Cook for 1 hour and 30 minutes. Get the pork out and add the pineapple slices over the pork and also make sure to wet with broth.

6. Bake for an additional 30 minutes.

7. Serve with Dijon mustard and your favorite side.

Nutrition Information per serving: 397 Cal, 27.5 g total fat 2.5 g carb., 42.4g protein

Spicy Mexican Style Stuffed Poblanos

Ingredients:

Ghee (for cooking)

½ onion (yellow, diced)

3 garlic cloves (minced)

1 lb. beef (lean, ground)

1 6oz. can of tomato paste

1 6oz. can of green chilies (diced)

½ Tbsp. garlic powder

1/8 tsp. paprika

2 Tbsp. hot sauce

Pepper (as desired)

¼ tsp. red pepper (ground)

Salt (as desired)

Directions:

1. Preheat the oven to 350 degrees.

2. Warm the ghee on medium-high heat, in a large-sized skillet.

3. Toss the onions and garlic in. Cook until the onions become clear. Add in the beef and cook it until it has browned.

4. Add in the tomato paste, green chilies, garlic powder, paprika, hot sauce, pepper, red pepper, and salt.

5. Slice off the tops of each poblano pepper and remove the seeds. Rinse the insides of each out. Cut a line down the side of each pepper and then stuff the meat mixture inside each pepper.

6. Set the peppers on a baking pan and cover with foil.

7. Bake for about 25 minutes.

Nutritional Informations: Calories 310, Carbs 15 g, Fat 17 g, Protein 25 g

Delish Mushroom

Ingredients:

2 cups sliced fresh mushrooms

1 minced garlic clove

1 Tbsp. olive oil

3 cups turkey or chicken broth

1 Tbsp. Almond flour or arrowroot

3 cooked slices of bacon (crumbled)

Salt and pepper

Directions:

1.   In a large pot, heat the olive oil and cook the minced garlic for 5 minutes.

2.   Add the mushrooms for another 5 minutes.

3.   Finally, add the broth of your choice and bring to boil. Cover next and let the soup simmer for 20 minutes.

4.   Use the blender next to get the desired consistency of cream. If you want a thicker soup, whisk arrowroot in some broth in a separate bowl and mix it with the rest of the soup, it will help.

5.   Include also the bacon gradually in the blender and make sure they blend well.

6.   Do not over salt. Taste before serving.

Nutrition Information per serving: 199 Cal, 5.1 g total fat 6.1 g carb., 6g protein.

Garlic Turkey Soup

Ingredients:

2 chopped celery stalks

2 chopped green onions

1 sliced large carrot

3 minced garlic cloves

4 cups turkey broth

2 Tbsp. lime juice

1 Tbsp. soy sauce

½ tsp. dried ginger

1 tsp. dried cilantro

1 Tbsp. Cayenne pepper

Salt

Olive oil

Directions:

1.   In a large pot, heat the olive oil and cook the garlic, green onions, and celery for 5 minutes.

2.   Add the carrot and cook an additional 5 minutes.

3.   Next it's time for the turkey broth, soy sauce, lime juice and spices. Let it simmer for a good 20 minutes.

4.   For the last 10 minutes, add the shredded turkey and make sure to serve warm.

Nutrition Information per serving: 256 Cal, 11.2 g total fat 9.5 g carb 9.5g protein.

Creamy Almond Celery

Ingredients:

5 cups chopped celery (no leaves)

2 cups of turkey or chicken broth

1 cup almond milk

2 chopped green onions

½ tsp. celery salt

½ tsp. dried basil

Black pepper

Directions:

1. Simply add all the ingredient in a large pot.

2. Bring to boil and then lower temperature and let it simmer for about 40 minutes.

3. Blend the soup until the texture is satisfying.

4. Verify the seasonings and add pepper of needed.

Nutrition Information per serving: 130 Cal, 1.6 g total fat 7 g carb., 2.9g protein.

SPICY SAUSAGE SOUP

Ingredients:

3 cooked turkey sausages (you can use your favorite kind)

1 chopped yellow onion

2 minced garlic cloves

1 cup almond milk

1 cup turkey broth

1 peeled and chopped sweet potato

½ jar of spicy salsa (your favorite brand)

½ Tsp. Cayenne pepper

½ smoked paprika

1 tsp. dried cilantro

Salt

Olive oil

Directions

1.   In large pot, cook the garlic and onion using olive oil.

2.   Next, add the broth, almond milk, and salsa with all the seasonings. Let it cook on low for about 15 minutes.

3.   While the soup is simmering, prepare the sausages, by cooking them thoroughly in a skillet with a drizzle of olive oil.

4.   Remove the soup from heat. Let it cool down some and blend it until is a smooth texture.

5.   Serve with a few slices of sausages in each bowl.

Nutrition Information per serving: 280 Cal, 7.7 g total 6 g carb, 19.1g protein.

Sweet Potato Curry Soup

Ingredients:

- 3 peeled and diced sweet potatoes
- 2 cups beef broth
- 1 cup unsweetened coconut milk
- 1 minced shallot
- 2 tbsp. maple syrup
- 2 tsp. curry powder
- 1 tsp. sea salt
- 1 tsp. chili powder
- 1 tsp. sweet paprika

Directions:

In a large pot over medium-high heat, add your sweet potatoes to your beef broth. Cook for around 10 minutes or until all of your sweet potatoes are fork tender.

Once your sweet potatoes are tender, mash them in to the broth with a potato masher.

Once you have mashed your sweet potatoes, add in the rest of your ingredients to the pot and cook for around 10 minutes or until everything is heated through.

When your soup is heated through, take it off the heat and use an immersion blender to smooth it out before serving.

Nutrition Information: 340 calories, 12.8g fat, 35g carbs, 25g protein

Garlic Avocado Chicken Salad Wraps

Ingredients:

- 2 peeled, mashed avocados
- 1 juiced lime
- 2 tbsp. chopped fresh basil
- ½ tsp. garlic salt
- ½ tsp. black pepper
- 4 cups chopped cooked chicken
- ¼ cup raisins or sultanas
- ¼ cup chopped walnuts
- 2 heads worth of lettuce leaves

Directions:

In a mixing bowl, combine your avocados with your basil, lime juice, pepper, and garlic salt and using a fork, mash them together.

Once your avocado mixture is well combined and mashed, add in your raisins or sultanas, chicken, and walnuts and stir with a silicone spatula to mix your ingredients together well.

Lay out your lettuce leaves and spoon your chicken salad in to them and roll up.

Nutrition Information: 470 calories, 20g fat, 21g carbs,42g protein

Asparagus Bamboo Beef

Ingredients:

1 pound grass fed ground beef

1 can bamboos shoots (drained)

3 cups cut asparagus

½ chopped yellow onion

2 Tbsp. olive oil

1 Tbsp. fish sauce (Paleo friendly)

1 Tbsp. apple cider vinegar

1 minced fresh ginger

Salt, pepper

Directions:

1.   This dish is basically like a stir fry but made with ground beef. So start by cooking the onion in a little olive oil in a skillet.

2.   Meanwhile boil water and cook for 10 minutes the asparagus, cut them in half.

3.   In the skillet, add the beef, some salt and pepper and cook for 10 minutes, making sure the beef stays crumbly.

4.   Add the rest of the ingredients, including the asparagus so you can finish off the dish and cook until the beef is completely done, maybe another 12 minutes or so.

5.   Serve hot.

Nutrition Information per serving: 230 Cal, 8.5 g total fat 6.9 g carb., 9.9g protein.

Walnut Chicken in Lettuce Wraps

Ingredients

- 1 lb. chicken breast
- 1/2 cup pomegranate seeds
- 1 lemon juiced
- 1/4 cup walnuts, chopped
- 8 large Romaine lettuce leaves
- Extra virgin olive oil

Directions

1. Slice chicken breast into thin strips.
2. Place 2 tbsp. olive oil in skillet and sauté chicken until golden brown.
3. Add nuts and pomegranate seeds, sauté for two minutes.
4. Squeeze lemon juice on top, cover and allow to cool.
5. lay down two pieces romaine lettuce and spoon chicken pomegranate chicken into leaves and roll into wrap.

Nutrition Information: 347 calories, 22g fat, 14g carbs, 39g protein

Paleo Pesto Chicken

Ingredients

- 1 lb. chicken breasts, boneless, skinless
- 1 onion, diced
- 8 cloves garlic,
- 1 cup fresh basil
- ¼ cup pine nuts
- ½ cup cashews, soaked overnight
- ½ cup water
- 1 tsp. salt, pepper
- Extra virgin olive oil
- 4 cauliflower wraps

Directions

1. Preheat oven to 375 degrees and coat baking dish with olive oil.

2. Place basil, garlic, pine nuts, cashews, salt, pepper, water and ¼ cup olive oil in food processor and mix until smooth, set aside.

3. Place chicken in baking dish and coat with ¾ of basil mixture, bake in oven for 30 minutes turning halfway.

4. Slice chicken into strips, place on wraps and spoon a little remaining basil mixture in each wrap.

Nutrition Information: 390 calories, 22g fat, 11g carbs,36g protein

Tasty Mussels Soup

Ingredients:

4 pounds mussels (cleaned)

1 Tbsp. olive oil

2 chopped green onions

3 minced cloves garlic

1 chopped yellow bell pepper

4 chopped celery stalks

3 cups vegetables broth

1 cup water

1 cup diced tomatoes

1 Tbsp. lemon juice

1 tsp. garlic powder

1 tsp. Cayenne pepper

Sea salt

Directions:

1.   In a large pot heat the olive oil and cook the onions and garlic.

2.   Add next the pepper, celery, and lemon juice, and mix well.

3.   Finally add the rest of the ingredients: vegetable broth, water, diced tomatoes, Cayenne pepper, garlic powder, and salt.

4.   Bring to boil. Add the mussels and cook for about 10 minutes.

5.   Serve with fresh parsley and lemon wedges.

Nutrition Information per serving: 279 Cal, 11.5 g total fat 9.5 g carb., 16.5g protein.

Paleo Chicken Giblets Healthy Soup

Ingredients:

1 pound chicken gizzards (ask your butcher)

3 minced cloves garlic

2 chopped green onions

2 sliced large carrots

2 cups chicken broth

3 cups of water

Salt and pepper

1 tsp. garlic powder

1 tsp. oregano

2 Tbsp. olive oil

Fresh parsley

Directions:

1.   Heat the olive oil in a saucepan and brown the giblets or gizzards you have purchased for about 15 minutes.

2.   Add the garlic, green onions, carrots and all seasonings. Cook for 5 additional minutes.

3.   Add the chicken broth and water and bring to a boil.

4.   Let it simmer on low temperature for 50 minutes.

5.   Serve with fresh parsley on top.

Nutrition Information per serving: 310 Cal, 17.5 g total 9.5 g carb., 21.5g protein.

Carrots Beef Stew

Ingredients:

- 1 ½ lbs. beef stew meat cubed

- 2 tbsp. butter (grass-fed)

- 1 largely cubed onion

- 1 ½ cups baby carrots

- 1 ½ cups diced potatoes (sweet potatoes if you prefer)

- 3 dry bay leaves

- 1 can (10.75 oz.) tomato soup

- 1 ½ soup cans of water

- 1 tbsp. steak sauce

- 1 packet (1 oz.) of dry onion soup

- ½ tsp. lemon pepper seasoning

Directions:

In a slow cooker, add your beef and butter. On top of the beef, add in your carrots, onion, potatoes and bay leaves.

In a mixing bowl, combine your steak sauce, water, tomato soup, and onion soup mix. Once they are well mixed, add the liquid ingredients in to the slow cooker and throw your lemon pepper seasoning on top.

Cover your slow cooker and cook on low for 8 to 10 hours until your beef is tender.

Nutrition Information: 282 calories, 11.3g fat, 22g carbs,23g protein

Balsamic Coconut Chicken

Ingredients:

4-8 chicken drumsticks (depending on size)

2 tbsp. coconut oil

¼ cup fresh chopped rosemary

1 chopped red onion

¼ cup maple syrup

½ cup balsamic vinegar

4 diced fresh peaches – pitted and peeled

Salt and pepper

Directions:

1.   Preheat the oven to 350 degrees F.

2.   Heat the coconut oil in the skillet and cook the red onion, and then the peaches, cook for 10 minutes.

3.   Add the maple syrup, the rosemary, salt, pepper and balsamic vinegar. This will be your delicious sauce for your chicken.

4.   In a baking dish, place the chicken drumsticks and pour the sauce all over them.

5.   Bake in the oven for about 45 minutes to an hour.

6.   Make sure to remove them half way through, and stir the sauce and moisten the chicken.

7.   Serve on cauliflower rice.

Nutrition Information per serving: 269 Cal, 7.2 g total fat 18.3 g carb, 21.6g protein

Black Pepper Cauliflower Soup

Ingredients:

- 2 tbsp. butter (grass-fed)

- 1 cup chopped onion

- 5 cups cauliflower chopped

- 2 chopped garlic cloves

- 5 cups low sodium chicken broth

- 1 tsp. sea salt

- ¾ tsp. black pepper

- 1 tsp. white truffle oil

Directions:

In a large soup pot, melt your butter. Once melted, add in your onions and cook until they are tender.

When your onions are tender, stir your garlic in to the onions and then add your cauliflower. Cook until your cauliflower is softened. Add your chicken broth and salt and pepper in to the pot and stir to mix well.

Cover your pot and allow your soup to simmer for 25 minutes or until your cauliflower is completely fork-tender.

After 25 minutes, take your soup off the stove and use an immersion blender to blend until smooth. Drizzle the top of each bowl with your truffle oil before serving.

Nutrition Information: 142 calories,7g fat, 12g carbs,7.9g protein

Garlic Chicken Lemon With Cabbage

Ingredients

- 1 lb. chicken breasts, roasted
- 1 red bell pepper, seeded, chopped
- 1 celery stalk, finely chopped
- 1 onion, peeled and chopped
- 4 cloves garlic
- 1 lemon, juiced
- 1/2 head cabbage
- 1 tsp. salt, pepper

Directions

1. Heat large pot of water until boiling.

2. Separate cabbage leaves and place in boiling water for two minutes, remove and run under cold water.

3. Chop chicken breasts into ½" pieces, place in large bowl and mix with remaining ingredients save cabbage.

4. Spoon chicken mixture into cabbage leaves and secure roll with toothpick or enjoy open faced.

Nutrition Information: 246 calories,10g fat, 5g carbs,35g protein

Delicious Tropical Mango Chicken

Ingredients:

- 1 lb. chicken breasts
- 1/2 cup mango, chopped
- 1/4 cup parsley, chopped
- 2 tbsp. coconut cream
- 1 tsp. paprika
- 1 tsp. salt, black pepper
- Extra virgin olive oil
- 4 almond wraps

Directions

1. Combine mango, parsley, coconut cream in bowl, set aside.

2. Slice chicken breast into strips.

3. Heat 2 tbsp. olive oil in skillet; add chicken breast and sauté until golden brown.

4. Sprinkle with paprika, salt, pepper and spoon into wraps.

5. Top with mango chutney and roll them up.

Nutrition Information: 320 calories,12g fat, 19g carbs,35g protein

Onion Stir Fried Pork

Ingredients:

- 1 lb. thinly sliced pork tenderloin
- 4 chopped garlic cloves
- 1 tbsp. chopped ginger
- ½ cup chopped cilantro
- ¼ cup plus 2 tbsp. olive oil
- 2 sliced yellow onions
- 1 sliced red bell pepper
- 1 tbsp. lime juice
- ½ cup chopped cilantro

Directions:

In a ceramic mixing bowl, combine ½ cup cilantro, ¼ cup olive oil, garlic, and ginger. Mix the ingredients well and then add in your pork loin. Mix everything together to coat your pork loin with your ingredients evenly.

Once your pork loin is covered evenly, cover the bowl and set it in the refrigerator to marinade overnight

The next morning, take your pork and marinade from the fridge and take the pork out of the marinade. Shake the pork well over the bowl to let any extra marinade drip off. Throw out your marinade.

In a large skillet, heat 1 tbsp. of olive oil on high heat. Once the olive oil is hot, add your onions and stir as they cook. Cook until your onion is soft and then add in your red bell pepper. Stir the onion and pepper and let it cook for 3 minutes.

After 3 minutes, add your pork in to your skillet, pour in your lime juice, and throw in ½ cup of your cilantro. Allow this mixture to cook while stirring. Once your cilantro begins to wilt, take the mixture off the heat and serve.

Nutrition Information: 306 calories,16g fat, 14g carbs,22g protein

Ginger Broccoli Chicken

Ingredients:

- 2 cubed skinless, boneless chicken breasts

- 2 tbsp. olive oil

- ¼ plus ½ cup honey

- 2 tbsp. chopped ginger

- 2 chopped red bell peppers

- 1 yellow onion cut in to 8ths

- 1 head of broccoli chopped

- 1 cup peeled, cubed fresh pineapple

Directions:

In a large skillet, heat your olive oil over medium heat. Once your oil is hot, add in your chicken, ginger, and ¼ cup of your honey. Stir the ingredients well and allow to cook until your chicken is golden.

When your chicken is golden, add in your broccoli, bell peppers, onion, the remaining honey, and pineapple. Stir again to combine your ingredients together.

Cover your skillet and cook until all of your vegetables are fork tender while stirring throughout cooking. Serve.

Nutrition Information: 309 calories,6.7g fat, 30g carbs,19g protein

Brown Sugar Garlic Chicken

Ingredients:

- 8 skinless chicken thighs
- 2 sliced onions
- 4 crushed garlic cloves
- 2/3 cup apple cider vinegar
- 1/3 cup low sodium soy sauce
- 1 tbsp. brown sugar
- 1 dry bay leaf
- Black pepper to taste
- 2 tsp. smoked paprika
- 1 head bok choy cut in strips
- 2 sliced green onions

Directions:

Take out your slow cooker, throw in your apple cider vinegar, onions, garlic, brown sugar, soy sauce, and bay leaf and mix well to combine. Throw in black pepper to

taste.

Now, place your chicken thighs on top of the ingredients in your slow cooker and dust the paprika over the chicken.

Cover your slow cooker and cook on low heat for 8 hours until your chicken is thoroughly cooked.

After 8 hours, turn your slow cooker on to high heat and then throw in your bok choy. Stir to combine your ingredients again, cover the slow cooker and cook for 5 more minutes.

Portion out your chicken mixture and top with green onions before serving!

Nutrition Information: 450 calories,20g fat, 25g carbs,39g protein

Best Paleo "Pizza"

Ingredients:

- 2 lbs. extra lean ground beef (if possible, grind your own)

- 2 eggs

- ½ cup grated parmesan cheese

- 12 oz. shredded mozzarella cheese

- 1 cup tomato sauce

- 3.5 oz. pepperoni slices

- 1 tbsp. salt

- 1 tsp. caraway seeds

- 1 tsp. oregano

- 1 tsp. garlic salt

- 1 tsp. black pepper

- 1 tsp. red pepper flakes

Directions:

Begin by pre-heating your oven to 450 degrees.

While your oven pre-heats, take a mixing bowl and add together your caraway seeds, salt, garlic salt, oregano, red pepper flakes, and black pepper. Mix these dry ingredients together well.

In a separate mixing bowl, combine your eggs and beef and use your hands to mix them together thoroughly. Throw your dry ingredients you just mixed in to your meat mixture. Add in your parmesan cheese as well. Mix these ingredients together well.

Grease a 12" x 17" baking pan and press your beef in to the pan as evenly as possible.

Once your oven is pre-heated, bake your dish for 10 minutes or until the meat is not pink anymore. Remove your dish from the oven and drain off any excess grease.

Now, lower the rack in your oven until it is 6" from the heating element and switch on the broiler.

Dust your meat with 1/3 of your mozzarella cheese, then pour your tomato sauce over the cheese. Now dust another 1/3 of your mozzarella cheese over the tomato sauce. On top of the second layer of mozzarella cheese lay out your pepperoni and then cover it with the rest of your mozzarella.

Put your pizza dish in to the oven and broil it until your cheese is golden brown. Remove from the oven, cut and serve!

Nutrition Information: 500 calories,25g fat, 5.1g carbs,59g protein

Yummy Paleo Turkey Burgers

Ingredients:

- 2 lbs. ground turkey
- 1 chopped Granny Smith apple
- ¼ cup chopped mushrooms
- 3 chopped scallions
- 3 tbsp. paleo approved BBQ sauce
- 2 tbsp. spicy mango chutney (store bought)
- 2 tbsp. red pepper jelly
- 2 shakes Worcestershire sauce
- 1 dash sea salt
- 1 dash garlic powder
- Black pepper to taste
- 16 paleo sandwich rounds (not included in nutritional information)

Directions:

Begin by turning your grill on to medium heat and make sure that the grill grate is oiled just enough to stop your burger from sticking.

While your grill heats, take a large mixing bowl and combine all of your ingredients together. Use your hands to mix everything together well. Once mixed, form 8 patties out of the mixed ingredients and set them on to a plate.

Cook your burger patties on the grill until they are cooked through.

Once cooked, put your turkey burger patty between your paleo sandwich rounds and eat as a burger!

Nutrition Information: 206 calories,8.6g fat, 10g carbs,22.8g protein

Thyme Bacon Chicken

Ingredients:

- 4 slices bacon
- 3/4 lb. chicken breast, skinless, boneless
- 2 Granny Smith Apples, peeled, chopped
- 1 lemon, juiced
- 1/2 tsp. thyme
- 1 tsp. salt, black pepper
- Extra virgin olive oil
- 4 flax tortillas

Directions:

1. Coat 4 qt. slow cooker with olive oil.
2. Place apples in bottom of pot, top with chicken, bacon and spices.
3. Cook on low overnight for 8 hours.

Nutrition Information: 318 calories,18g fat, 10g carbs,35g protein

Coconut Lemon Stir Fry Shrimp

Ingredients:

- 24 large deveined, peeled shrimp

- ½ cup lemon juice

- 1 chopped yellow onion

- ½ cup olive oil

- 3 minced garlic cloves

- 1 tbsp. lemon zest

- 1 tbsp. grated ginger

- 1 tsp. ground turmeric

- 1 tbsp. coconut oil

Directions:

In a large mixing bowl, combine your onion, lemon juice, garlic, olive oil, ginger, lemon zest, and turmeric. Mix these ingredients together well to combine them. Once mixed, put your shrimp in to this mixture, cover the bowl and set it in the fridge overnight to let the shrimp marinade.

The next morning, take the shrimp mix from the fridge. Scoop out the shrimp from the marinade and set the marinade aside.

Over medium-high heat, melt your coconut oil in a large skillet. Once melted, add your shrimp to the skillet and cook until they are cooked through. When the shrimp are cooked through, pour the reserved marinade in to the skillet and continue stirring while the marinade comes to a boil.

Serve with the heated marinade.

Nutrition Information: 388 calories, 21.7g fat, 5.9g carbs,21g protein

Slow Cooker Ground Ginger Spiced Pork Loin

Ingredients:

- 2 lbs. cubed boneless lean pork loin

- 2 tbsp. potato starch

- ½ cup freshly squeezed orange juice

- 1 tbsp. curry powder

- 1 tsp. granulated chicken bouillon

- ½ tsp. ground ginger

- ¼ tsp. ground cinnamon

- ½ tsp. salt

- 1 peeled, cored, diced Granny Smith apple

- 1 chopped yellow onion

- 1 minced garlic clove

- ¼ cup raisin

- ¼ cup unsweetened flaked coconut

- 2 tbsp. cold water

Directions:

Take out your slow cooker and throw in your orange juice, chicken bouillon, curry powder, cinnamon, ginger, and salt. Mix these ingredients together well to disperse them.

Add in your Granny Smith apple, garlic, onion, coconut, and raisins, and stir again. Next, set your pork on top of the ingredients you have already added to your slow cooker.

In a small mixing bowl, whisk your potato starch and water together thoroughly until you no longer have any lumps left. Once you have a smooth mixture, stir it in to your slow cooker mixture.

Put the lid on your slow cooker and cook on low for 6 hours, or until your pork is tender and cooked through.

Nutrition Information: 216 calories,10g fat, 12.5g carbs,18.9g protein

Paleo Zucchini Jambalaya

Ingredients:

- 1 lb. peeled, deveined, cooked shrimp
- 1 lb. cooked, chopped, and cooled chicken breast
- 1 cup low sodium chicken broth
- 1 tsp. hot sauce
- 2 tbsp. Cajun seasoning
- 2 diced zucchinis
- 3 seeded, diced green bell peppers
- 1 can (14 oz.) crushed tomatoes
- 6 chopped cloves of garlic
- 2 vertically halved andouille sausages cut in to ¼" chunks

- 1 diced yellow onion

- 1 tbsp. butter (grass-fed)

- 1 tbsp. olive oil

Directions:

In a large pot over medium heat, heat up your butter and olive oil. Once your butter has melted, throw in your andouille sausage and onion. Stir and cook these ingredients until your onions begin to turn brown.

Once your onions have browned, add in your garlic and stir to mix thoroughly. Cook for 2 minutes and then add in your crushed tomatoes, zucchini, green bell pepper, hot sauce, Cajun seasoning, and chicken broth. Stir to mix thoroughly and allow your ingredients to come to a boil.

As your ingredients come to a boil, turn down your heat to let the mixture simmer. Let this pot simmer until all of your liquid has evaporated, making sure to stir periodically to prevent sticking to the pan. It will take about 15 minutes for the liquid to cook off.

After your liquid has cooked off, add in your shrimp and your chicken, stir, and leave on the heat until your shrimp and chicken are warm.

Nutrition Information: 260 calories,8.5g fat, 14.5g carbs,31g protein

Yummy Thai Lime Pork

Ingredients

- 1 lb. pork tenderloin
- 1 onion, sliced
- 2 limes, juiced
- 1 tsp. salt, black pepper
- 8 large lettuce leaves
- Extra virgin olive oil

Directions:

1. Preheat oven to 400 degrees, lightly coat baking tray with extra virgin olive oil.

2. Slice tenderloin into 1" pieces and toss with lime juice, salt pepper.

3. Place tenderloin into oven to cook for 30 minutes.

4. Place lettuce leaves on flat surface, spoon a little tenderloin per lettuce leaf, top with onion slices, roll and secure with toothpick.

Nutrition Information: 360 calories, 10 fat, 14.5g carbs,45g protein

Salmon Burgers

Ingredients:

- 7.5 oz. wild Alaskan salmon cooked and chopped
- ¼ cup almond meal
- 3 eggs
- 2 tbsp. olive oil
- Salt and pepper to taste
- 8 paleo sandwich rounds (not included in nutritional information)

Directions:

In a bowl, combine your salmon, eggs, almond meal, salt and pepper, and 1 tbsp. olive oil. Use your hands to mix your ingredients together well and then make 4 patties. Set your patties aside.

In a skillet over medium heat, heat 1 tbsp. of your olive oil and cook your patties until they are heated all the way through and browned on the outside.

Serve as is, or serve them between two paleo sandwich rounds if you like!

Nutrition Information: 230 calories,15g fat, 2.3g carbs,19g protein

Broccoli Turkey Sausage

Ingredients:

- 4 sliced Italian turkey sausage links

- 3 tbsp. olive oil

- 2 minced garlic cloves

- 2 trimmed bunches broccoli rabe

- Lemon zest to taste

- Dash of red pepper

- Sea salt to taste

- ½ lemon

Directions:

In a large skillet, heat a little of your olive oil on medium heat – enough to coat the bottom of the skillet.

Once your olive oil is hot, add your sausage slices and cook them until they are brown. Once the sausage is browned, add in your garlic and cook for a minute or so, while stirring. Be careful that your garlic doesn't burn.

Now add in your broccoli rabe and stir to mix. Add lemon zest to your skillet to your taste, and then throw in a dash of red pepper and a dash of sea salt. Mix together to coat your broccoli rabe.

Cook for 15 minutes until your broccoli rabe is wilted. Once wilted, squeeze your lemon over your ingredients in the pan.

Plate your turkey sausage, broccoli rabe mixture and serve.

Nutrition Information: 560 calories,25g fat, 15g carbs,30g protein

Yummy Coconut Mustard Creamy Crab

Ingredients:

- 2 cups crab meat
- 1 celery stalk, chopped
- 1/2 cup cashews, soaked overnight
- 2 tbsp. coconut cream
- 1/2 tsp. dry mustard
- 1 lemon, juiced
- 1 tsp. cayenne
- 1 tsp. each salt and pepper
- Extra virgin olive oil
- 4 cauliflower wraps

Directions:

1. Place cashews in food processor and mix until crumbly, add coconut cream and mix until smooth, add a little water if required.

2. Mix cashew with crab meat, celery and spices.

3. Spoon into cauliflower wraps.

Nutrition Information: 129 calories,10g fat, 5g carbs,10g protein

Mayonnaise Crab Cakes

Ingredients:

- 1 lb. fresh lump crab meat
- 1 egg
- 2 tbsp. mayonnaise
- 1 tsp. Dijon mustard
- ½ tsp. Worcestershire sauce
- ¼ tsp. Tabasco sauce
- ¼ tsp. lemon juice
- 1 ½ tsp. seafood seasoning
- Black pepper to taste
- ¼ cup almond flour
- 1 tbsp. diced red pepper
- 2 tsp. sliced green onion
- 1 tbsp. chopped parsley
- 1/3 cup almond flour

Directions:

Begin by greasing a baking sheet.

In a mixing bowl, combine your mayonnaise, egg, Worcestershire sauce, Dijon mustard, lemon juice, Tabasco sauce, seafood seasoning and black pepper. Stir together using a silicone spatula making sure to mix everything thoroughly together.

In a clean bowl, put your crab meat and then pour your egg mix in to the meat. Use your hands to mix the crab meat and egg mixture together. Once mixed well, add in your peppers, ¼ cup of your almond flour, red pepper, parley, and green onions. Use your hands to mix all of your ingredients together again.

Now, break your mixture in to six even portions and use your hands to make a patty with each portion of your ingredients. Set your patties aside.

In a clean bowl, drop the rest of your almond flour. Take each of your patties and cover them in the almond flour and put them on your baking sheet.

Put your patties in to the refrigerator for an hour.

Once the patties have finished chilling in the refrigerator, preheat your oven to 400 degrees. When the oven has pre-heated, bake your crab cakes for 20 minutes or until the cakes are golden brown in color.

Nutrition Information: 114 calories,6.8g fat, 4.3g carbs,9.7g protein

Dill Onion Shrimp Salad

Ingredients

- 1 lb. medium shrimp, peeled, deveined
- 1/4 cup dill, chopped
- 1 small red onion, chopped
- 2 tbsp. coconut cream
- 1 tsp. salt, pepper
- 1 egg, hard-boiled
- 4 flax tortillas

Directions

1. Place dill, coconut cream, salt, pepper and egg in blender and mix until creamy.

2. Mix dill sauce with shrimp, red onion and wrap in flax tortillas.

Nutrition Information: 140 calories,3g fat, 4g carbs,25g protein

Chapter 8 PALEO DESSERTS RECIPES

Yummy Cinnamon Banana Cake

Ingredients:

Bottom Layer

1 large sliced banana

2 Tbsp. coconut oil

2 Tbsp. chopped pecans

1 tbsp. Honey

1 tsp. cinnamon

Top layer

2 medium eggs

1/3 cup honey

½ tsp. baking soda

1 tsp. apple cider vinegar

1/3 cup coconut milk

½ cup coconut flour

1 mashed large banana

Directions:

1.   Preheat oven to 350 degrees F.

2.   Spread evenly the melted coconut oil in the bottom of a cake pan. Then sprinkle the cinnamon on top.

3.   Place a layer of sliced bananas and add the chopped pecans also. Set aside.

4.   In a large bowl combine all the ingredients listed under "top layer. Mix well and then pour the batter on top of the first one. Spread evenly with a spatula.

5.   Bake for about 25 to 30 minutes in the oven.

6.   Once you are ready to remove the cake from the pan, Place it upside down, it will be pretty ad yummy at the same time.

Nutrition Information per serving: 183 Cal, 5.9 g total fat 27.5 g carb., 3g protein.

Chocolate Pineapple Coconut Bars

Ingredients:

½ cup almond flour

½ cup macadamia nuts

½ tsp vanilla extract

4 tbsp raw cacao powder

5 dates

1 ½ tsp coconut oil, melted

For the filling:

1 cup fresh pineapple, chopped

1 tbsp lime juice

1 tbsp raw honey

½ tsp salt

2 eggs

1 ½ cup shredded coconut, unsweetened

1 tbsp vanilla extract

½ cup almond flour

Directions:

Make the crust. Combine the almond flour and cacao powder in a large mixing bowl. Blend the nuts in the food processor. Remove the pits and process until creamy. Add the coconut oil, vanilla and dates to the dry ingredients. Use your hands to combine the mixture. Spread it at the bottom of the pan lined with wax paper.

Make the filling. Beat 2 eggs in a bowl. Add in the pineapples, shredded coconut, lime juice, honey and vanilla. Mix with a spatula. Spread the mixture on top of the crust then sprinkle with the shredded coconut. Bake for 20 minutes at 350 degrees until done. Allow to cool before your slice.

Nutrient facts: 204 calories, 13 g fat, 11 g net carbs, 5 g protein

Delicious Blueberry Cream Pie

Ingredients:

3 cups almonds

½ cup honey

1 tbsp lemon zest

½ tsp salt

½ tsp cinnamon

2 tbsp coconut oil

1 tsp almond extract

For the filling:

2 tsp plant based gelatin

2 tbsp water

1/3 cup honey

4 cups blueberries

1/3 cup lemon juice

1 can coconut milk

Directions:

Place the cinnamon and almonds in your blender and process until the desired texture is reached. Some people like smooth dough while others prefer to have some texture in it. Add the rest of the crust ingredients. Blend well to combine.

Make the filling by combining the water and gelatin together. Stir to combine. Add the lemon juice and stir. You can place the mixture on hot water if it gets to clumpy. Pour the coconut milk to a mixer. Add the honey. Whip until soft peaks form. Add the gelatin to the whipped cream. Pour it on top of the crust. Place in the refrigerator for 4 hours until it is set.

Top with blueberries and then serve.

Nutrient facts: 382 calories, 24 g fat, 40 g net carbs, 7 g protein

Honey Coconut Cheesecake

Ingredients:

3 cups dates, soaked in warn water and pitted

1/3 cup coconut flour

1/8 tsp salt

1 cup coconut oil, melted

1/3 cup coconut, shredded

For the filling:

1 ½ cups raw honey

1 cup coconut oil

6 tbsp tapioca starch

¼ tsp salt

Coconut flakes for garnish

1 ½ cups coconut butter

5 cups frozen raspberries

1 ½ tsp vanilla extract

Fresh raspberries for garnish

Directions:

Melt the coconut oil by placing the container on very hot water. Prepare the crust first. Preheat the oven at 325 degrees. Place the dates in a food processor.

Add in the melted coconut oil. Blend until paste is formed. Scrape the sides of the processor. Mix the coconut flour, salt and shredded coconut in a bowl. Add the date paste and stir. Place in a pan and press down using a spatula. Bake for 30 minutes until it hardens a little bit.

Make the filling. Mix the cocoa butter, frozen raspberries, oil and honey in a saucepan. Place over low heat. Stir and cook until it is warm. Transfer to a blender.

Mix in the salt, tapioca starch and vanilla. Blend for a minute then pour on top of the crust.

Place in the refrigerator for 12 hours to cool. Remove from the pan and top with raspberries and coconut flakes.

Nutrient facts: 223 calories, 5.8 g fat, 35 g net carbs, 1 g protein

Vanilla Peach Coconut Donut

Ingredients:

5 medjool dates, pitted

3 eggs

¼ cup coconut flour

1 tbsp cinnamon

½ tsp salt

1 tbsp water

1 tsp vanilla

¼ cup coconut oil, melted

¼ tsp baking soda

½ cup peaches, diced

For the glaze:

¼ cup coconut butter

1 tsp vanilla

1 peach, cored and sliced

2 tbsp honey

Dash of cinnamon

Directions:

Preheat the donut hole maker. Mix the dates with water. Heat the mixture for 30 seconds. Remove from the heat and mash with a fork to make a paste.

Add the eggs and vanilla then pour the mixture to the food blender. Add the remaining ingredients except for the peaches. Process it until all ingredients are incorporated. Add in the peaches.

Add the right amount of batter to the donut hole maker and follow manufacturer's instructions.

Make the glaze by mixing the peaches, honey, vanilla, butter and cinnamon in the food processor. Let it cool then dip the donut holes into the glaze to coat.

Nutrient facts: 90 calories, 5 g fat, 8 g net carbs, 1.6 g protein

Ginger Banana Carrots Muffins

Ingredients:

1/2 cup almond flour

1 1/2 cups shredded carrots (I choose the baby carrots but you can choose the regular size ones also)

1/2 cup coconut flakes

1 tsp. ground ginger

1 tsp. baking soda

4 large eggs

1 tsp. vanilla

1/4 cup coconut oil

1 large ripe banana

1/2 cup chopped cashews or walnuts

1/2 cup unsalted grass-fed butter

1 Tbsp. honey

Directions:

1.   Preheat the oven to 350 degrees F.

2.   First, combine in a bowl the following: flour, carrots, coconut flakes, ginger, and baking soda.

3.   In a different bowl, combine the eggs, vanilla and coconut oil very well.

4.   In the dry mixture with the carrots, add the bananas and mx well. Gradually incorporate the wet (eggs) mixture and mix all together. Finally add the chopped nuts.

5.   Then, pour the muffin batter in greased muffin tins and bake in the oven for about 30 minutes.

6.   Meanwhile, whip the butter and honey and set aside.

7.   This will serve as frosting for your muffins, so you can really serve them as carrot cakes.

Nutrition Information per serving: 185 Cal, 7.5 g total fat 4.5 g carb., 3g protein.

Yummy Fruits Salad

Ingredients:

2 cups cubed watermelon

2 cups cubed cantaloupe

1 cup fresh raspberries

1 cup halved green grapes

1 cup fresh cubed pineapple

Directions:

1.   Simply combine all ingredients in a bowl and mix well. You can add or remove any fresh fruits you like.

Nutrition Information per serving: 115 Cal, 1.5 g total fat 17.5 g carb, 3g protein.

Almond Coconut Donuts

Ingredients:

1/2 cup almond flour

1/4 cup coconut flour

1/2 tsp. baking soda

½ tsp. salt

5 large eggs

½ cup agave syrup

1 Tbsp. pure almond extract

¼ cup coconut oil

½ tsp. all spices

Directions:

1.   Preheat the oven to 350 degrees F.

2.   Combine all the dry ingredients in a large bowl (flour, baking soda, all spices, and salt).

3.   Add the eggs, agave syrup, coconut oil, and almond extract.

4.   Combine very well together, if you would rather use an electronic mixer instead of a simple spatula, go ahead.

5.   You will use a donut pan to fill each space with the batter and then bake for about 22 minutes. Don't overfill.

6.   You could sprinkle some coconut sugar on the donuts if you like.

Nutrition Information per serving: 174 Cal, 3.9 g total ,14.5 g carb, 4.1g protein.

Peanut Butter Vanilla Honey Truffles

5 tbsp sunflower butter

1 tbsp raw honey

¾ cup almond flour

½ tsp salt

1 tbsp cacao butter

1 tbsp coconut oil

2 tsp vanilla extract

1 tbsp flaxseed meal

¼ cup chocolate chips

Chopped almonds for garnish

Directions:

Stir the jar of sunflower butter before using. Place the flaxseed meal, honey, almond flour, butter, vanilla and salt in a large bowl. Use your hands to stir all of the ingredients.

Roll the dough into balls and place on top of parchment paper. Place in the refrigerator for half an hour.

Melt chocolate chips then add the cacao butter. Dip the truffles into the chocolate and sprinkle with almonds. Refrigerate until firm.

Nutrition facts: 74 calories, 5 g fat, 3.9 g net carbs, 2.2 g protein

Delicious Triple Fat Fudge

Ingredients:

½ cup ghee

¼ cup coconut oil

¼ cup cocoa powder

¼ tsp stevia

¼ cup ghee or butter

¼ cup cocoa butter

1 tbsp raw honey

1 tsp vanilla

Directions:

Gently melt the cocoa butter in a saucepan. Add the ghee, coconut oil and coconut spread. Stir well to combine. Add in the vanilla, stevia and honey. Whisk well to combine.

Mix in the cocoa powder and whisk. Remove it from the heat and keep whisking to smooth all the lumps.

Pour the mixture on a medium sized pan that has been lined with parchment paper. Place in the refrigerator for 2 hours.

Once it is solid, pull the parchment paper to easily lift the fudge. Cut into small squares and serve.

Nutrient facts: 303 calories, 33 g fat, 3 g net carbs, 1 g protein

Maple Syrup Apple Cookies

Ingredients:

1 cup unsweetened almond butter

1/2 cup maple syrup

1 egg

1 tsp baking soda

1 small red delicious diced apple

½ tsp cinnamon

½ tsp. ground ginger

Directions:

1.   Preheat oven to 350 degrees F.

2.   In a bowl, combine the cashew butter, maple syrup, egg and baking soda. Stir well.

3.   Add the diced apples and the spices, mix again.

4.   On a greased baking sheet, place about 8-12 teaspoons about an inch apart.

5.   Bake for about 12 minutes.

6.   Let them cool for 5 minutes at least before eating one.

Nutrition Information per serving: 115 Cal, 4.5 g total 4.5 g carb., 2.9g protein.

Paleo Fruity Nuts Skillet

Ingredients:

1 large diced sweet potato

½ cup water

1 cup coconut milk

3 Gala diced apples

2 cups fresh blueberries

½ cup coconut oil

1 Tbsp. coconut sugar

½ tsp. Cinnamon

½ tsp. ground ginger

½ cup pine nuts

Directions:

1.   Preheat oven to 400 degrees F.

2.   Peel and dice the sweet potato first and start boiling the water and milk together.

3.   You will cook the potato ahead separately from the fruits for about 20 minutes in the boiling milk-water.

4.   Then in a skillet, heat some coconut oil and cook the apples by adding also the coconut sugar and spices.

5.   Once the sweet potato is cooked, add to the apples and ad also carefully the blueberries and mix well. Pour some of the cooking milk if needed.

6.   Serve warm.

Nutrition Information per serving: 189 Cal, 7.5 g total fat 13.5 g carb, 5g protein.

Special Fruit Cake

Ingredients:

Cake

3 cups tapioca flour

1/3 cup coconut oil

½ cup raw maple syrup

½ cup coconut milk

4 Tbsp. orange juice

½ tsp. baking powder

1 cup fresh blueberries

Topping

1 tbsp. orange zest

1/3 cup raw maple syrup

1/3 cup grass fed butter

Glaze

2 Tbsp. orange zest

1/3 cup raw honey

1/3 cup coconut oil or ghee

Directions:

1. Preheat the oven to 350 degrees F.

2. Mix the tapioca flour baking powder, and then add the orange juice, the coconut milk, and eggs.

3. You should stir some, but I highly recommend you stick all ingredients in the food processor for better constituency.

4. Also add the coconut oil and maple syrup slowly to the mix.

5. Pour the mix back in a bowl and carefully add the blueberries.

6. Pour the batter into the greased baking dish you set aside and bake for about 50 minutes.

7. Meanwhile, mix the ingredients for the glaze and once the cake comes out, pour generously on the cake.

Nutrition Information per serving: 275 Cal, 7.5 g total fat 17.5 g carb., 3g protein

Paleo Delight Caramel Pudding

Ingredients:

1 Fresh coconut (make sure you purchase the one with a white inside)

1 cup apricots (soften in boiling water)

2 Tbsp. honey

1 Tbsp. pure vanilla extract

Directions:

1. Now you can purchase the fresh coconut and remove the top and scoop out the inside.

2. Either way, place the coconut in the blender with the coconut water found.

3.   Meanwhile, you have let the apricots sit after pouring boiling water on them to soften them.

4.   Add the apricots in the blender as well as the honey and the vanilla.

5.   Blend again. Add water if needed.

6.   Serve in individual bowls.

Nutrition Information per serving: 115 Cal, 3.5 g total fat 6.9 g carb., 2g protein.

Honey Banana Cupcakes

Ingredients:

Grass fed butter for greasing

12 dates

3 tbsp coconut flour

2 eggs

½ tsp baking powder

10 tbsp water

1 ½ ripe banana, peeled and chopped

1 tbsp vanilla extract

1tsp honey

For the date ganache:

½ orange, juiced

1 tsp vanilla extract

Fresh raspberries for garnish

5 dates, chopped

3 tbsp almond milk

1 tsp honey

Directions:

Set the oven at 185 degrees. Grease your muffin tins with grass fed butter. Set aside. Place dates and water in a saucepan. Simmer over low heat until it breaks down and thickens.

Mash the mixture using a fork. Place banana, baking powder, vanilla, flour and egg in a blender. Process until combined. Add the dates to the banana. Stir to combine. Scoop it into the ramekins. Bake for 20 minutes.

Combine the ganache ingredients in a pot. Simmer for 4 minutes until the dates are tender. Mash with fork and whisk. Let the muffins cool before spreading the ganache on top. Add a few raspberries for garnish.

Nutrient facts: 203 calories, 4.5 g fat, 30 g net carbs, 4.2 g protein

Walnut Apple Cinnamon Coffee Cake

Ingredients:

½ cup almond flour

2 tbsp coconut flour

1 tbsp cinnamon

¼ tsp salt

2 eggs

1 tsp vanilla

¼ cup arrowroot starch

1/3 cup coconut palm sugar

1 tsp baking soda

1 tbsp butter

½ cup sour cream

1 cup grated apple

For the topping:

½ cup almond flour

2 tbsp coconut palm sugar

½ tsp salt

1 ½ cups walnut

4 tbsp melted butter

1 tbsp cinnamon

Directions:

Set oven at 350 degrees. Coat the baking pan with butter. Make the topping. Process the walnuts in the food processor. Add the rest of the topping ingredients and blend a few more times to combine.

Wipe your food blender and add the dry cake ingredients. Blend to combine. Cut the butter into smaller chunks and add to the ingredients. Pulse until the mixture resembled pie crust.

Combine the wet cake ingredients. Add the grated apple. Add to the food processor. Pour the mixture into the baking dish and sprinkle the topping. Bake for 30 minutes until done.

Nutrient facts: 402 calories, 35 g fat, 9 g net carbs, 11 g protein

Almond Coconut Dates Balls

Ingredients:

1 cup chopped dates

2 medium eggs

½ cup. Maple syrup

1 tsp. almond extract

¼ cup grass fed butter

2 cups chopped walnuts or chopped pecans

1 cup shredded coconut

Directions:

1.　Combine the eggs, the maple syrup and the grass fed butter in a small pot on medium heat.

2.　Bring to boil and continue cooking on low heat for 10 minutes.

3.　Turn off the heat and add the almond extract. Set aside.

4.　In a bowl, mix the chopped dates and the chopped chosen nuts.

5.　Add the syrup and then roll them into small balls.

6.　Finally, dip each ball in the shredded coconut and refrigerate the balls until ready to serve.

Nutrition Information per serving: 109 Cal, 8.5 g total 11.1 g carb, 5g protein.

Tasty Fruity Dip

Ingredients:

1 cup fresh strawberries,

1 cup almond milk

1 Tbsp. orange juice

2 tbsp. honey

Directions:

1. In the blender combine the fruits and the almond milk, honey and orange juice.

2. Activate until the texture becomes really smooth.

3. Serve chilled with your favorite fruits or even some veggies if you like.

Nutrition Information per serving: 92 Cal, 4.5 g total fat 9.2 g carb., 2g fiber, 2g protein

Strawberry Banana Sorbet

Ingredients:

- 1 ripe banana
- 2 cups fresh strawberries
- ½ cup coconut cream

- 1 teaspoon agave nectar

Directions:

Simply combine all ingredients and blend.

Place in the freezer and take it out when it is solid but not completely frozen. Scoop it out and place in a glass.

Place a fresh strawberry as an edible decoration and there you have it!

Nutrition Information: 106 calories,3g fat, 4g carbs,25g protein

Honey Pumpkin Cake Cookies

Ingredients:

¾ cup pumpkin puree

5 eggs

2 tbsp honey

½ tsp baking power

½ tsp nutmeg

1 cup dark chocolate chips

¼ cup coconut oil, melted

1 tsp vanilla extract

1/3 cup coconut flour

1 tsp cinnamon

¼ tsp ground cloves

Directions:

Set your oven to 375 degrees.

Combine the puree, eggs, honey, oil and vanilla in a large bowl. Whisk the ingredients to combine. In a separate bowl, add the baking powder, coconut flour and spices.

Add the spices to the pumpkin mixture. Stir until the mixture is free of lumps. Add the chocolate chips. Line the baking sheet with parchment paper. Scoop 2 tablespoon of dough and drop on the baking sheet.

Flatten and then bake for 10 minutes until done. Allow it to cool for 10 minutes before serving.

Nutrient facts: 115 calories, 7.6 g fat, 9 g net carbs, 3 g protein

Nutritious Spinach Brownies

Ingredients:

1 ¼ cups frozen spinach, chopped

6 oz semisweet chocolate

½ cup palm shortening

1 tbsp honey

½ cup cocoa powder

¼ tsp baking soda

½ tsp cream of tartar

1 cup pureed green plantain

½ cup extra virgin coconut oil

6 eggs

1 tbsp molasses

1 tbsp vanilla

½ tsp salt

½ tsp cinnamon

Directions:

Set the oven at 325 degrees. Cover the baking pan with wax paper. Place a small saucepan on top of a stove then melt the chocolate and coconut oil. Mix in the vanilla and stir to incorporate. Let it cool.

Combine the cream of tartar, baking soda, cinnamon, salt and cocoa powder. Whisk to combine.

Place the honey, spinach, egg, molasses and plantain in the food processor. Blend until the mixture is smooth. Add the palm shortening and blend well until everything is incorporated.

Add the chocolate to the egg mixture and continue the blending process. Add the dry ingredients and stir to combine. Pour the batter to the pan. Spread the mixture using a spoon or spatula.

Bake for 40 minutes. Let it cool then cut into squares.

Nutrient facts: 112 calories, 8 g fat, 8 g net carbs, 2 g protein

Delicious Honey Coconut Bars

Ingredients:

1 cup coconut flakes

1/cup raw honey

½ tsp. almond extract

¼ tsp. salt

Directions:

1.   Mix simply all the ingredients listed above in the food processor.

2.   Then press the mixture into a dish and refrigerate for several hours before cutting into bars.

Nutrition Information per serving: 108 Cal, 4.5 g total fat 7.5 g carb., 3g protein

Delight Nutmeg Fruity Cobbler

Ingredients:

8 cups of mix strawberries and pomegranate (frozen works well)

½ cup coconut sugar

1 Tbsp. honey

¼ cup arrowroot powder

Topping:

1 1/2 cup coconut flour

¼ cup coconut sugar

2 small eggs

½ cup melted grass fed butter

½ tsp. ground nutmeg

Directions:

1. Preheat the oven at 350 degrees F.
2. In a bowl, place the frozen fruits and let them thaw.
3. Add the coconut, sugar, honey, and the arrowroot. Mix well, of course.
4. In a second bowl, combine the coconut flour, sugar, nutmeg.
5. Finally, whisk the eggs and butter together in a third bowl.
6. Stir the eggs mixture into the dry one and mix well.
7. In a greased baking dish pour the fruits mixture first and then the batter.
8. Bake for about 25 minutes

Nutrition Information per serving: 219 Cal, 5.1 g total fat 17.3 g carb., 3g protein

Desserts Waffles

Ingredients:

2 large ripe bananas

4 eggs

½ tsp baking soda

2 tsp almond extract

2 Tbsp. coconut oil

Pinch cinnamon

Strawberries, blueberries, blackberries, bananas or any other fresh fruits you enjoy on your waffles

Directions:

1.   Place the bananas and the eggs in the blender and activate until it starts being smooth.

2.   Add the rest of the ingredients and then continue processing.

3.   You will be left with the waffle batter that is smooth and not too thick, not too liquid.

4.   Use you waffle make as instructed and pour the batter.

5.   Top with your favorites.

Nutrition Information per serving: 179 Cal, 4.5 g total fat 11.5 g carb., 3g protein.

Chapter 9 PALEO SMOOTHIES RECIPES

Delight Chocolate Paleo Smoothie

Nutrition Facts

Per Serving

Factors	Amount
Calories	358
Protein	5 g
Fat	8 g

Ingredients

- 1 pound pitted dates (organic)
- 3 ½ cups of unsweetened almond milk (organic)
- 5 to 6 ripe bananas (small and organic)
- 4 tablespoons of raw and cocoa powder (organic)

Directions:

1. Slice and to freeze bananas or use already frozen banana slices. Mix all the ingredients and place on a baking sheet in a single layer

Vanilla Pumpkin Smoothie

Ingredients:

½ cup pumpkin

1 cup unsweetened almond milk

½ small banana, frozen

½ tablespoon Raw honey

½ teaspoon vanilla extract

¼ teaspoon cinnamon

1/8 teaspoon ginger

1/8 teaspoon nutmeg

1/8 teaspoon ground cloves

1/8 teaspoon allspice

Handful of ice

Directions:

Blend the ingredients together until smooth.

Nutrition Facts: Calories 160; Total Fat 3.2 g Protein 3.0 g; Vitamin A 392%; Vitamin C 17%; Calcium 50%; Iron 15%\

Coconut Macadamia Coffee Smoothie

Nutrition Facts

Per Serving

Factors	Amount
Calories	202.5
Protein	6 g
Fat	18 g
Carbohydrates	29 g
Fiber	4 g
Sugar	12 g

Ingredients

- 3/4 cups organic coconut milk
- 1/2 cup cold coffee
- 1/4 cup avocado (organic)
- 1/4 cup organic macadamia nuts
- 1/4 cup ice cubes
- 2 scoops stevia / raw organic honey to the taste

Directions

1. Blend all the ingredients using a blender until a smooth form is made.

2. Use almond flakes and a few macadamia nuts to garnish and for an added texture.

Banana Pineapple Smoothie

Ingredients:

2 cups pineapple juice

2 cups strawberries

1 banana

1 cup diced peaches

Ice cubes

Directions:

Blend the ingredients together until smooth.

Nutrition Facts: Calories 178;   Total Fat 0.5g Protein 2.2g; Vitamin A 4%; Vitamin C 144%; Calcium 4%; Iron 6%

Strawberry Almond Smoothie

Ingredients:

1 frozen banana

8 strawberries

2 Tablespoons almond butter

1 Cup Almond Milk

2 Cups Spinach

Nutrition Facts: Calories 177; Total Fat 5.3g Protein 5.2g; Vitamin A 57%; Vitamin C 75%; Calcium 8%; Iron 9%

Spinach Berry, Banana Smoothie

Ingredients:

1 cup Spinach

10 frozen Strawberries

½ cup frozen blueberries

1 cup coconut milk

1 teaspoon honey

1 Banana

Directions:

Blend the ingredients together until smooth.

Nutrition Facts: Calories 413; Total Fat 8 g Protein 4.1g; Vitamin A 29%; Vitamin C 117%; Calcium 6%; Iron 19%

Almond Milk Mango Smoothie

Ingredients:

1 Mango, peeled

1 cup frozen strawberries

1 banana

1 cup Almond milk

Ice

Directions:

Blend the ingredients together until smooth.

Nutrition Facts: Calories 350; Total Fat 3. Protein 3.4g; Vitamin A 44%; Vitamin C 203%; Calcium 50%; Iron 11%

Paleo Macadamia & Poppy Seed Smoothie

Nutrition Facts

Per Serving

Factors	Amount
Calories	213
Protein	5 g
Fat	5.4 g
Fiber	3 g

Ingredients

- 1 cup organic coconut water

- 1/2 cup organic almond milk

- 1 organic frozen ripe banana (or 1 organic ripe banana with some ice cubes)

- 1 tablespoon desiccated coconut (organic)

- 1 tablespoon raw cocoa powder (organic and unsweetened)

- 1/2 teaspoon pure vanilla paste (organic)

- 1/2 teaspoon poppy seed paste (organic)

- 1 teaspoon macadamia powder (organic)

- 1/2 teaspoon of cinnamon spice

Directions

1. Use a blender to blend all the ingredients until the desired smooth form is attained.

2. Put it into your smoothie serving glasses.

3. Optionally, glasses can be garnished with desiccated coconut and macadamia nuts as topping.

Cocoa Coffee Banana Yogurt Paleo Smoothie

Nutrition Facts

Per Serving

Factors	Amount
Calories	225
Protein	4 g
Fat	47 g
Carbohydrates	37 g
Fiber	2 g
Sugar	14 g

Ingredients

- 2 ripe bananas (organic)
- 1 cup almond milk (organic)
- 1 cup organic frozen yogurt (fat free)
- 1 cup coconut cream (light whipped)
- 1/2 cup chilled coffee
- 2 tablespoons unsweetened cocoa powder (organic)

Directions

1. Blend all the ingredients except whipped cream in a blender and until a smooth consistency in achieved.

2. Transfer it into a serving glass and use the light whipped coconut cream top it.

3. For a strong flavor of the coffee, enjoy the smoothie without the extra toping with the cream.

Avocado Pineapple smoothie

Ingredients:

1 mango, peeled

2 cups kale

2 cups fresh pineapple

¼ avocado

1 small banana

2 kiwis, peeled

Handful of ice

Directions:

Combine all the ingredients in a blender and blend until smooth.

Nutrition Facts: Calories 348; Total Fat 8.9g Protein 8.2g; Vitamin A 417%; Vitamin C 526%; Calcium 24%; Iron 18%

Orange Spiced Pineapple Smoothie

Ingredients:

1 Banana

1 ½ cups Pineapple

1 Orange

One Lime, juiced

1 Tablespoon ginger

½ teaspoon nutmeg

2 teaspoons turmeric

½ cup coconut milk

¾ cup water

Directions:

Combine all the ingredients in a blender and blend until smooth.

Nutrition Facts: Calories 254; Total Fat 4.5g ,Protein 3.3g; Vitamin A 5%; Vitamin C 94%; Calcium 6%; Iron 14%

Avocado Pineapple Surprise Smoothie

Ingredients:

1 avocado

1 ½ cups pineapple

1 egg yolk

1 ½ cup coconut milk

2 teaspoons lime juice

Ice cubes

Directions:

Puree all the ingredients in the blender until smooth. Add ice until desired consistency.

Nutrition Facts: Calories 474 Total Fat 4 .3g   Protein 5.7g; Vitamin A 5%; Vitamin C 54%; Calcium 5%; Iron 16%

Macadamia Avocado Coffee Smoothie

Nutrition Facts

Per Serving

Factors	Amount
Calories	260
Protein	5 g
Fat	5 g
Carbohydrates	8 g
Fiber	8 g
Sugar	5 g

Ingredients

- ½ cup cold coffee

- 2-3 dates

- ½ cup avocado

- ¼ cup macadamia nuts

- ¾ cup coconut milk

- ¼ cup of ice

Directions

1.　　Blend all the ingredients in a blender and until a smooth consistency in attained.

Refreshing Apple, Lemon Detox Smoothie

Ingredients:

1 apple, with peel

1 lemon, juiced

1 cup kale

1 stalk of celery

1/3 cup fresh parsley

1 tablespoon chia seeds

¼ teaspoon cinnamon

1 cup water

Directions:

Combine all the ingredients in a blender and blend until smooth.

Nutrition Facts: Calories 156 Total Fat 5.2g Protein 5.0g; Vitamin A 122%; Vitamin C 122%; Calcium 23%; Iron 21%

Spinach Lemon, Mango Smoothie

Ingredients:

½ lemon, juiced

1 mango, peeled and sliced

½ apple, peeled and sliced

2 cups spinach

½ cup water

Directions:

Combine all the ingredients in a blender and blend until smooth.

Nutrition Facts: Calories 213; Total Fat 1.4g Protein3.4g; Vitamin A 146%; Vitamin C 182%; Calcium 10%; Iron 13%

Pineapple, Spinach Smoothie

Ingredients:

1 cup fresh pineapple

½ lemon, juiced

1 cup spinach

¼ teaspoon fresh grated ginger

Nutrition Facts: Calories 145; Total Fat 0.5g Protein 2.9g; Vitamin A 59%; Vitamin C 120%; Calcium 7%; Iron 10%

Healthy Kale Coco Nutty Paleo Booster

Nutrition Facts

Per Serving

Factors	Amount
Calories	220
Protein	17 g
Fat	3 g

Ingredients

- 1 cup organic coconut milk
- 1/2 cup organic pineapple (frozen or fresh)
- 1 cup baby spinach

Directions

1. Add all the ingredients in a blender and blend everything until totally smooth.

Honey Strawberry Rhubarb Smoothie

Ingredients:

1 ½ cup frozen strawberries

1 ½ cup rhubarb, chopped

1 ½ Tablespoon Raw Honey

2 cups almond milk

Blend all the ingredients together. Add more Honey if more sweetness is desired.

Nutrition Facts: Calories 165; Total Fat 2. Protein 1.9g; Vitamin A 12%; Vitamin C 80%; Calcium 39%; Iron 7%

Mango & Coconut Carrots Smoothie

Nutrition Facts

Per Serving

Factors	Amount
Calories	155
Protein	8 g

Fat   6 g

Carbohydrates   38 g

Fiber 5 g

Ingredients

- 1 cup organic carrots (peeled and sliced)
- 1 cup coconut milk
- 1 medium mango (sliced)
- 1 cub organic vanilla yogurt
- 2 tablespoons raw honey (pure)
- 2 cups ice cube

Directions

1.   Blend all the ingredients using a blender until a smooth form in reached.

Banana Clementine Strawberry Smoothie

Nutrition Facts

Per Serving

Factors	Amount
Calories	165
Protein	2 g
Fat	0 g

Carbohydrates   39 g

Fiber 12 g

Ingredients

- 2 clementine (organic)
- 1 small ripe banana (frozen and sliced)
- 8 ounces strawberries (fresh or frozen)
- ginger to taste (freshly sliced)

Directions

1. Peel and seed organic clementine.

2. Blend all the ingredients in a blender and until a smooth texture is attained.

Detox Lemon Cucumber smoothie

Ingredients:

1 Tablespoon Lemon Juice

1 Tablespoon Lime Juice

1 Cup Cucumber, Peeled

1 Tablespoon Avocado

Handful of Spinach

Sea Salt

Black Pepper

Handful of Ice

Directions:

Add all the ingredients to a blender. Blend until smooth. Add salt and pepper to taste. The salt and pepper will soften the bite from the lemons and limes.

Nutrition Facts: Calories 37;   Total Fat 2.0g ,Protein 1.0g; Vitamin A 3%; Vitamin C 18%; Calcium 2%; Iron 2%

CONCLUSIONS:

Thanks again for downloading my book, I hope you have enjoy it, and hope you find it relevant what you are looking for .

Practice Paleo diet will benefits you a lot of things, leading to a better , healthier .

If you've enjoy my book, would you please kindly leave a a positive review on amzon , thanks so much in advance .

Good Luck!

Made in the USA
San Bernardino, CA
10 July 2017